MW00834313

YOU ARE THE PRIZE

Arnold,
thank you so much for
your amazing support
throughout these years.
I hope you will always
know you are the prize!

[signature]

YOU ARE THE PRIZE

SEEING YOURSELF BEYOND THE IMPERFECTIONS OF YOUR TRAUMA

AMNONI MYERS

NEW DEGREE PRESS

COPYRIGHT © 2021 AMNONI MYERS

All rights reserved.

YOU ARE THE PRIZE

Seeing Yourself beyond the Imperfections of Your Trauma

ISBN   978-1-63676-502-0 *Paperback*
            978-1-63676-018-6 *Kindle Ebook*
            978-1-63676-118-3 *Ebook*

This memoir is dedicated to you. Yes, you, the reader.
Always remember that you are the prize.

CONTENTS

*There is no greater agony than bearing
an untold story inside you.*

—MAYA ANGELOU

A NOTE OF INSPIRATION

"Each of us is here now because in one way or another we share a commitment to language and to the power of language, and to the reclaiming of that language which has been made to work against us. In the transformation of silence into language and action, it is vitally necessary for each one of us to establish or examine her function in that transformation and to recognize her role as vital within that transformation."
—Audre Lorde

The pace of working at the White House is exhilarating. People are coming and going all around you, at all hours, and there is a constant buzz. You get to meet and work with people who want to make the world a better place. Amnoni was no different. And just like everybody else, some days were better than others.

I distinctly remember the look on Amnoni's face that day. I couldn't tell you the exact day, or the exact reason, but I remember the conversation. I just knew when she looked up from her desk that something was a little different that day. I recognized that look—the one where you half-smile your way into trying to convince others you're doing just fine when, in fact, you feel as though you're falling apart on the inside. I knew that what I most needed to do at that moment was invite Amnoni into the hallway for one of our "walk n' talks."

I jumped at the chance and asked, "Amnoni, do you have a moment? I'd like your advice on something. It'll only take a few minutes, and we can walk together to my next meeting."

Amnoni looked around at the other interns with whom she shared an office, stood right up, and said, "Sure, I've got a few minutes."

Amnoni and I had the pleasure of serving our country while working together at the White House during the Obama Administration. I was a Senior Policy Advisor working on a broad portfolio of domestic policies while simultaneously awaiting confirmation into a role that Amnoni shared—deep interest in child welfare reform. Over the course of working together, we shared little pieces of our stories, exchanged ideas, and shared dreams of a better future for children, youth, and families who struggled.

As soon as Amnoni emerged from the office to join me in the hallway and was out of earshot of the others, I quickly turned to her and didn't mince words.

"What's up? Looks like you're having a rough day."

She looked up at me, chuckled, and said, "How'd you know?"

"I recognize that look because I know how it feels. What's really going on?"

Amnoni looked at me, puzzled. She took a deep breath as we descended one of the Eisenhower Executive Office Building's grand spiral staircases and said, "Sometimes, I just don't feel like I belong here. I just don't fit in."

People continued to rush past us, a constant flow of energy, but we were already deep into our conversation, lost in our own little world. We grabbed a quick cup of coffee and continued our walk and talk back upstairs. As I listened to Amnoni describe what she was experiencing, we pulled over to a corner within a bird's-eye view of the doors that lead to the West Wing of the White House. Through those doors, I shared her experience of sometimes feeling isolated, overwhelmed, and like an imposter, all while working at the White House.

"Wait, what? *You* feel that way, too?" she asked.

«All the time," I replied.

For a few minutes, we compared notes on what it meant to feel lost, to live with imposter syndrome, and what we could do as colleagues to support each other in the daily grind. The dynamic of our relationship changed in that moment. I asked Amnoni to look down at the black limestone and white marble flooring and pointed out the fossils in some of the tiles. She hadn't noticed them before. And just like the storied history of how those fossils made their way into this national landmark, or the countless stories of ambassadors, secretaries, vice presidents, presidents, diplomats, and unsung heroes who have walked those very halls, so, too, did Amnoni belong.

They all had a place in history. Whether publicly recognized or not, their very presence in the building mattered in the course of our collective history. And not only did Amnoni belong in the White House at that very moment in time, but she made it and all of us stronger and better by reminding us why we were called to serve the least among us. She used the power of her words, of her own story and truth to remind those around her of our responsibility to act, to transform our silence into action.

And this is what makes Amnoni's words in this book so impactful today. She transforms the personal and silent into the public and powerful. She helps us understand that many of us struggle, and that despite the challenges we face, success is within our reach. From her journey to make sense of her childhood and complex family dynamics, to understanding just how beautiful, wanted, and loved she is as an adult. *You Are the Prize* offers us a vulnerable and honest glimpse into a life that remains full of hope, promise, and potential. Reflecting back on that moment in the hallway sometime in the spring of 2015, I also remember how Amnoni and I parted ways.

After chatting for a few more minutes, I looked straight at her and said, "You've got this. And *no* one belongs here more than you do at this moment!"

She took a deep breath and that extraordinary smile of hers re-emerged. She held her head high, and she replied, "Thank you. I've got this!"

And within seconds, she turned around to head back to her office. Just then, as if on cue, the automatic doors opened and natural light flooded the hallway, engulfing Amnoni on her path.

Amnoni's story is one beautiful piece of our many American stories. We must continue to listen and learn from each other's stories, especially when working with children, youth, and families who are survivors of trauma in their lives. We can truly begin to understand each other only through respecting and meeting people where they are—in this way, we can develop the trust we so desperately need to create the world for which we all yearn.

Rafael López

Former Commissioner, Administration on Children, Youth, and Families

US Department of Health & Human Services

Former Senior Policy Advisor, the White House

AUTHOR'S NOTE

From an early age I knew I wanted to write a book, so I began my journey around twelve years old—right as I entered the foster care system. During a therapy session, I shared with my therapist that I wanted to write a book about my life, and she encouraged it by bringing a brand-new notebook and pen for me to begin with at our next session.

I started from the beginning of my journey writing out scenes of my childhood but became overwhelmed shortly and stopped. While I was not confident that I would live past the age of twenty-five, I also didn't realize how difficult it would be to write in detail about a life that I've managed to live.

Fast forward many years later; I find myself at a similar place. The journey of writing still hasn't been easy. In fact, it's been a journey fueled with grief, anger, sadness, transitions, and lots of questions, one being, "Should I continue writing this book?"

There were unspoken rules growing up in a community where the culture of silence is pervasive, and one of those rules—which you never should break—is "what happens in this house stays in this house." Even though I didn't hear those exact words, I knew from a very early age that, in order to protect my family, I had to stay quiet about the experiences happening to me and just "give it over to God" in hopes that it would all go away.

Truth is, childhood trauma just doesn't go away. You spend your adulthood unpacking and working through experiences that weren't your fault only to find out that life continues getting harder. Many have asked, "How did you get through your writing journey?" and to be honest, this is how:

- I've spent a lot of time snuggled in my bed
- I've spent a lot of time overthinking
- I've spent a lot of time crying
- I've spent a lot of time doubting myself
- I've spent a lot of time worried about deadlines
- I've spent a lot of time caring what others will think
- I've spent a lot of time thinking about my little sister and what she would want from me

In the midst of all of these feelings, I continued writing.

Make no mistake; while this book emphasizes that "you are the prize," I haven't always felt like the prize. My little sister and best friend, Ebony, is the person who shared these words with me during a difficult time in my life.

"Sis, always remember that you are the prize!" she exclaimed.

Since her passing, those words have sat with me, and each day I remind myself daily of who I am, embodying "being the prize." I also recognize that even if I don't always see myself as the prize or feel like I am, it doesn't mean I am not. Being the prize encompasses my inherent worth, dignity, and value as a human being. It means prioritizing my needs and caring for myself when things are easy and when they are tough. It means sharing my story despite how others may feel.

While this journey has not been an easy one, writing this book has empowered me to use my voice in ways I never imagined. I am no monolithic person. I was just a girl who went through the foster care system navigating struggles that almost every Black person navigates.

So what makes me so special? I often ask that question. Seeing the value that you bring into a space when you haven't always had a voice proves difficult, but the truth is my voice was there—it was just silenced. Through this writing process, I saw how my unique experiences brought me to where I am. I realized the person I worked so hard to un-become has shown me that I am monolithic in my own way.

Most importantly, this writing process has given me space to heal. In this process of unbecoming, I realize how important it is to honor my emotions and feelings, and I am learning it is okay to not always be okay.

My goal is for you to see yourself as the prize, knowing that all of your experiences hold meaning—not just for you, but for your community and for the people you encounter. My hope is that each of you are able to see your own light through the stories I share, knowing that healing is a life-long journey. As I come back home to myself, I hope the road you take will also lead you back home. Maya Angelou said it best when she said, "There is no greater agony than bearing an untold story inside of you."

And always remember: You are the prize!

PREFACE

At 4:07 a.m. the Secret Service is outside The Ritz Carlton in the heart of Washington DC, ready to pick me up and drop me off at the White House to introduce the First Lady, Michelle Obama.

My phone rings. A bit disoriented, I answer. "Hello—"

"It's Agent Braxton," the speaker cuts me off. "I'm your driver, Ms. Myers. It's time."

"I cannot believe this is happening," I mumble, stumbling into my clothes, barely missing slamming my shin on the corner of this too-big-for-one-person bed.

That's the Ritz for you: all pomp and circumstance, and yet no respect for a Black girl getting ready for her first ride in a Secret Service sedan to meet First Lady Michelle Obama—just kidding! Actually, I had to take the DC transit system because I was a broke intern. As I arrived at the White House, I thought to myself, *Never did I think I would be introducing Michelle Obama.*

I was a little girl who grew up without my parents, a young adult who struggled in my academic career because of a learning disability, and a young professional suffering from imposter syndrome. I arrived at the Executive Eisenhower building and began practicing my introduction of the

First Lady for "Take Our National Daughters and Sons to Work Day."

What made this moment extra special was seeing all the young Black and Brown foster youth sitting in the front row gazing at me, proud to see someone like them at center stage.

I'll never forget the moment I heard Michelle Obama's high heels hitting the floor as I saw a tall, Black, beautiful, and powerful woman approach. I couldn't believe it because, for the first time in my life, every teacher who told me I was learning too slowly and everyone who had ever told me that I wasn't good enough didn't matter. I felt worthy of being in that room. I had a knot in my stomach, but everyone reassured me that what I said was powerful.

It felt so good to see the First Lady cheer me on as I finished my introduction. I'll never forget hearing her speak to young people and saying with enthusiasm, "Like Amnoni says!"

Now I realize I am the prize, and I want other young people who have gone through what I've experienced to know the same.

Growing up in hoods like Dorchester, Mattapan, Hyde Park, and Roxbury, I was not surrounded by power, status, or elitism. I was just a young Black girl from Boston, and I didn't grow up with my parents. I experienced the foster care system, and I dealt with people telling me I would end up like my parents.

Somehow, I made it through to the other side. For the first time in my life, I felt iconic. I started an internship at the White House in the Domestic Policy Council on Urban Affairs, Justice, and Opportunity in 2015 under the Obama Administration. Working for the first Black president of our country gave me life. Now that we have a Black president in office, things should be better, right?

This was not the case.

Most other interns could do the unpaid internship without financial help, almost all of them White and privileged beyond belief. For someone who learned about this program through the Congressional Coalition of Adoption Institute, I felt like a fish out of water. Walking through the gates of Eisenhower's Executive Office Building everyday felt surreal. I saw Secret Service, cadaver dogs, the long red carpet—a dream for a girl like me. I pinched my cheeks daily to wake myself up to this newfound reality.

In the spring of 2015, I received an unexpected phone call from my little sister, Ebony. The call came at a perfect time, as I was looking forward to the much-needed break from my work day.

I could hear that Ebony—only twenty-five at the time, her voice clenched in fear—had tears streaming down her face. She was begging me for help.

"Sis, he's beating me!" she screamed.

Standing in that powerful building, alone and holding onto the pillars to keep it together, I imagined Ebony bruised and tattered as she lay on the floor.

Ebony never called me when she got a beating, but this time she had. I stood hopelessly, trying to hear every word, trying to catch the glimpses of her voice. Her abuser's yelling made it hard. I wished so badly that I could be there so I could rescue her. I stood in horror, hands shaking so badly I could barely hold the phone.

"Are you able to leave?" I stammered. "I'll stay on the phone as long as you need me."

I could hear him in the background screaming out, "You lazy hoe!" while his large fists jammed into her fragile body. I was powerless and afraid for her life. All I could do was listen as she begged me not to tell anyone. I wanted to tell someone, but I knew he would beat her even more if I did.

Minutes later, the phone went blank. After calling back several times, I no longer heard her voice on the other line. I was a wreck all day: I couldn't eat, and I was barely able to focus on work. I didn't know if I would ever hear her voice again, Thankfully, she called me that evening. This time, Ebony survived her injuries. Little did I know, a short two years later Ebony would lose her fight for survival to suicide.

Ebony felt her battles were invisible, but we could all see the surface of them. She thought we couldn't see her worth, but we could. A traumatic trajectory in her childhood led to years of substance abuse, mental health struggles, homelessness, and domestic violence. Ebony and I had grown up with the hope of raising kids together and growing old. We wanted to take care of each other, but Ebony's life was cut short, leaving nothing but memories, dreams, and hopes she and I never got to see.

Ebony's experience isn't uncommon. Her story propelled me in my efforts to advocate for better foster care.

While Ebony grew up in traditional foster home settings such as living with a foster parent, she also spent much of her time in group home facilities, which we know can have a devastating impact on a young person.

She moved around more times than I can count. Many other young people who went through foster care have this same story. There are approximately four hundred thousand children in the foster care system, and about twenty thousand young people age out of care annually, with few resources or support systems.1,2 The youth transitioning out of the foster care system are some of the most vulnerable and disadvantaged youth in the United States. While many teenagers celebrate their eighteenth birthdays or high school graduations, many others in the foster care system learn, at this time, that they may have to move out of their foster homes and begin adulthood immediately.

I'm inspired to write this book because I don't want my sister's and my stories to be silenced. Through our journeys, I want to bring a voice to so many other people's experiences. I want people to know what it means to overcome. Ebony and I grew up together. We did everything together, but because of an abrupt separation during foster care, our paths diverged. When we moved into the foster care system, I went one way and she went to another.

While my experiences helped me climb throughout my life, Ebony's life plummeted downwards. If she had been connected to the right resources, supports, and avenues, I believe she would still be here today. Even though it was her choice to take her life, Ebony talked about living without the pain and abuse she experienced on a daily basis. I wrote this book because I don't want any other young person to face what Ebony faced. I wrote this story about our lives to provide a pathway for others, so they know there is still life after death, even in the midst of grief.

In reading this book, I hope the rawness of our experiences helps you confront your challenges, grief, and losses, especially if you lost someone to suicide. I hope this book enables social policy leaders, child welfare leaders, and people who have access to young people's lives to build a new and better system that has families in mind first and foremost. I hope we can rethink how and why we remove children from their biological families and think about the immediate harm, stress, and pain it causes them. Just as important to also acknowledge are the stressors, challenges, losses, and trauma that happen later in life, so we can be better equipped to help these children and their families.

PART ONE

1988–2000

METAMORPHOSIS

As a little Black girl growing up, a sentiment that was strongly emphasized by my Great Aunt (affectionately known as Granma), family members, and the church, was to make sure you work every day to break generational cycles of poverty, addiction, and laziness.

Striving for Black excellence was imprinted upon me very early. "Don't end up like your mother and father," was a phrase I often heard.

This was sound advice at the time, given that I was brought up by an older Black southern woman who prized herself on being raised by strong parents, and by a father who was a pastor of an African Methodist Episcopal Church. Pictures of Rosa Parks, Langston Hughes, and Dr. Martin Luther King Jr. looked over at me while I watched TV from the floor. Despite these representations, I still had a limited understanding and scope of what it meant to go about breaking generational cycles when painful experiences in my childhood told me otherwise.

Because of my parents' drug use during the crack epidemic in the late 1980s, I was born with drugs in my system, had birth defects, and struggled with developmental delays throughout my life. Though Granma stressed that my siblings and I were born from a resilient lineage, both my mother and father were examples of what not to become.

As I've lived, their past trauma has trickled down onto my path, where I have experienced the impacts of generational trauma. I was in foster care from age twelve to eighteen, after my mother was charged with five counts of child abuse.

At eighteen years old, I was told I had to leave where I was living because my foster mom would not pay for my housing. I remember the day like it was yesterday because I'd just been laughing and making jokes with the college secretary, and in a blink of an eye, I found all my belongings on the front porch in black garbage bags. I had no warning, no extra time to process, not even a recommendation of how to navigate adulthood.

At that moment, I realized the system I relied on actually cared little about me or anything I did from that point on. I would have to navigate on my own with minimal support.

Despite the obstacles, I graduated from college with my bachelor's degree, interned on Capitol Hill and at the White House under the Obama Administration, and earned my Master's in Public Administration through the renowned National Urban Fellow Program in 2017 in New York City. My determination to overcome trauma and immeasurable support from mentors along the way helped me get where I am today.

Confronting My Past

During the fall semester of my senior year of undergraduate school, I was taking one of my last classes needed to graduate. I knew this moment was coming, as I dreaded having to complete one of the major assignments required by social work students. The first part of the semester focused on learning what a Genogram system is—a pictorial display of a person's family, relationship, and medical history—and the second part of the semester was completing it yourself. The Genogram system goes beyond the traditional family tree and digs deeper into one's family history to understand the hereditary patterns and psychological factors which help clinical social workers understand complex family dynamics. This system is often used to identify repetitive occurrences or behaviors using symbols to describe certain patterns and relationships.

As someone who had a complex history, I knew this task would not be easy; I actually dreaded it. Not only was I sweating bullets about getting in touch with family members to ask about difficult information, but it was also overwhelming to think about presenting such challenging information as a Black student in front of a class full of my White peers. I barely understood the full extent of my family dynamics, so how could they?

While navigating all of this, I struggled to embody the assignment because I was navigating an outdated Genogram system that did not have symbols reflective of other family structures, sexual orientation groups, and racial implications, such as historical trauma. While I was frustrated that I had to create my own symbols to understand my family history, I gained in-depth insight into the strong, resilient family I was unaware I had.

Through this process, I went on a personal journey of wanting to understand where my roots began outside of my mother's womb. I wanted to understand where my mother and father came from and what led them to become loveless parents.

The thought of rekindling a relationship with my mom was difficult, as I did not have a strong relationship with her at the time. Having to ask her about her family upbringing caused me to tread lightly so our relationship would not be strained any further. Luckily, we were able to survive the ordeal as my mother was very open about her life, and the life of her parents and siblings.

While it was easier to find information about my father's side of the family since I was raised by his aunt (Granma) for ten years, I was unaware she was suffering from early-onset dementia during this time.

Looking back, I cherish our weekly calls when Granma and I spent a number of hours on the phone together, listening to her share stories and anecdotes about our family history.

By speaking to both my mother and Granma, I learned there were patterns of abandonment, rejection, substance abuse, sexual abuse, and premature deaths in my family history. These themes extended beyond my generation, impacting both sides of my family. As shocking as it was, it made complete sense given that my ancestors had been stripped of their core, their families, and their talents, and then sold into slavery.

System Iniquities

The conditions my family had endured—oppression, racist policies, and a punitive system that takes children from their families—is a collective trauma African Americans have to live with.

These experiences are then funneled through children and young adults like Ebony, who was born into pain and died in pain as a result of a system that had failed her. The system has done little to acknowledge and accept the flaws of its creation, which has resulted in many young people struggling to thrive. One glimmer of hope in recent years has been shedding the bright light on the longstanding inequities in the child welfare system (Welch and Haskins, 2020).

The original intention for foster care was to be a temporary solution for families who struggled, but what it has become over the years is a permanent fixture with frail roots. For generations, Black families have been negatively impacted by the system meant to help them. Black and African American youth are overrepresented in foster care, comprising twenty-three percent of youth in care but only fourteen percent of youth in the US, according to the Annie E. Casey Foundation. Black youth are more likely to enter care, not be reunified with their families, move placements while in care, and age out of the system without a permanent placement such as adoption or reunification (Dettlaff, 2020). Even when families of color are referred for services, those services are not always available or accessible in minority communities (Child Welfare Information Gateway, 2021).

It has become easier for systems to blame birth parents and children for their downfalls without acknowledging the history that helped forge the destruction of their families. As I think about the path that Ebony and so many other young people went down, I realize how society perpetually sees and treats them as failures rather than children who are suffering from a lineage of trauma.

A Monarch Butterfly Emerges

At thirty-two years old, I am currently dealing with the repercussions of generational trauma through anxiety and Post-Traumatic Stress Disorder (PTSD). I suffer from feelings of abandonment because of lifelong loss of childhood, family separation, and a younger sister who took her own life.

This journey has shown me that resilience goes beyond what one can achieve or accomplish. Resilience begins in my DNA, traveling from the blood of my ancestors and into my veins. Despite being born into a world that has not always recognized the core of my being, I am breaking through the silos and finally seeing myself for who I truly am: I deserve love because I am the ultimate prize.

In this memoir, I will talk more in depth about the experiences I've faced as a foster care alumnus and how the trajectory of my path gave me the opportunity to see how I am the prize despite the negative things I've experienced.

CHAPTER 1:

CHAOTIC COCOON

I arrived on this earth with three strikes against me. I was born two months premature on June 16, 1988. My four-pound body kept a score of my mother's disease. I was subdued by the rhythm of her addiction; I was exposed to her dirty needles and the heroin that flowed through her dark veins. Cocooned in her belly without an escape and completely powerless, my father's violent grip almost became my demise with each of his strikes hitting my mother's womb with reckless abandon.

Bearing the weight of my parents' sins, my arrival into this world was met with withdrawal. The doctors tested me for controlled substances and quickly moved me to the Neonatal Intensive Care Unit (NICU) for immediate care. Before they could share my progress, my mother walked out of the hospital room and back into the streets—surrounded by a life she knew too well—and she never returned for me.

A child's identity is often rooted not only in genetics but in the presence of their parents. From one parent's wide eyes and broad nose to the other's dark complexion and personality traits, children go through life learning about the ways they are similar to their parents and the experiences they share. Typically, parents are present before and during birth, following each child through their most important milestones until death separates them.

For me, "parents" meant something radically different. For generations, abandonment, drugs, alcohol, and poverty plagued my family on both sides. I often questioned how I would be able to escape such a vicious cycle. I spent my life fighting to understand my worth because I was born into a world of circumstances that predetermined my life story before I could live it. Even though my parents may have wanted a better life for me, the strain of their rejection, neglect, and abuse made it difficult for me to heal.

The matriarch of the Myers family, my Aunt Edith, admirably took permanent custody of my brother, sister, and me, as an older adult, while also balancing being a daycare provider. She was affectionately known as "Granma" to her daycare community, family members, and grandchildren, so my siblings—Mallory and Ebony—and I followed suit.

While we were grateful for her role and presence in our lives, it was not enough to fill the void of still wanting our mother and father to be present. I imagined there was nothing better in the world than hearing family members tell you how much "you look just like your Mama," or "you are so smart, just like your Daddy," but I had never been able to witness such affirmations for myself.

Although both of my parents were alive and lived nearby even when they were incarcerated, my siblings and I still had little contact with them. As a child, I blamed myself for their absence. I didn't believe my parents wanted me. I often had negative thoughts like, *I mean, who has kids if they can't take care of them? Why didn't you just abort me? I would've been better off an egg.* I didn't realize how complicated parenthood actually was. I often took their rejection and abandonment personally.

Holidays, birthdays, and special occasions brought up their own unique anxiety—I wondered if anyone would show up for me.

Mother's Day

"Sasha. Brian. Keisha. Please come down to the front office," the gentle voice said over the intercom. "Your mothers have arrived."

I was about seven years old in the second grade. Today was the annual Mother's Day breakfast at my elementary school, and my peers and I eagerly awaited our parents' arrival.

Snickering and giddy, our excitement could be felt around our second-grade classroom as students' names were called. Even though I had little contact with my mom, I still held on to hope that she would arrive.

As I peeked outside the classroom door, the bouquet of barrettes all over my head was visible from the hallway—there was no way Mom could miss me. I envisioned us skipping hand in hand down the long hallway to the cafeteria to indulge in some brunch. But I knew this was all a made-up dream. I hoped maybe Granma would make it this time, at least. I hated missing out on these brunches, and thought it was a possibility that this year might be different.

Itching for my name to be called next, I paced back and forth in my classroom. I didn't want to be the last one called. I didn't want to face the embarrassment of having no one show up for me yet again. Kids would ask me all the time if my mom was going to show up—I hated that question.

One by one, student after student, kids left to meet their mothers in the gymnasium for the Mother's Day brunch. *Please, please, please come,* I thought, anticipating Granma's arrival, an answered prayer. I hoped she had found someone to watch her daycare kids, but as the clock kept ticking and the room became emptier, doubt crept in.

Fewer announcements trickled from the corner of the room where the announcement speaker rested. Soon it was just my teacher, Mrs. Stacy, and me.

Angry, sad, and disappointed, I stood by my cubby with my face toward the ground and my arms folded, a posture of safety. My cheeks grew warm as the back of my throat began to harden and tears silently rushed down my face.

"How come nobody came for me?" I asked. "This isn't fair."

Quietly, Mrs. Stacy moved in closer behind me and placed her hands on my shoulders, gently stroking my back in silence. She then slowly walked me back to my seat.

I still held out hope that someone would come, but that prayer was never answered.

Experiences like this were painful to say the least. I felt I was searching up and down the aisle for a Mother's Day card that didn't exist, opening the card to read meaningless words and lies about a love I craved but would never experience. There were no words to describe the pain; being slapped in the face with your mother's bare hand would be closer to the feeling than anything I could describe. One of the most painful losses I've experienced was losing someone who was still alive but didn't have the capacity to be in my life—like she was dead, nowhere to be found.

To pass through the unease of her existence, I often lied and said she was dead when "yo mama" jokes were handed out on the playground. Saying she was dead was easier than admitting my mother was a crackhead and a prostitute. I was ashamed of her past, and I carried that burden for most of my life.

A Meaningful Encounter

I grew up with only a vague awareness of my father, relying on the snippets Granma would often share with me. Like an oral history, Granma offered fragments about who he was. Through these fragments, Granma and other members of our community impressed upon my siblings and I very early on that we were not to follow in his footsteps. Instead, we were to "follow in the footprints of God."

"Just be more like Jesus," was often thrown at us as we sat on pews in the "Father's house." I struggled to know exactly how to do that without a father figure to show me. This Jesus character that Granma and the church talked about made things even more complicated.

Growing up in the African Methodist Church I knew Jesus wasn't white, but it was conflicting to see beaming white characters reflecting the sunlight in stained-glass windows around the sanctuary while we sang from our seats. *Is this Jesus real?* I often wondered. *How can he be if I can't even see him face to face?*

I wanted so badly to have faith, and I prayed on my knees every night before I counted sheep. But how was I supposed to understand the love of a father, like Jesus, when I had never met the person who had knocked my mother up?

Meeting My Father

Are we there yet? I repeated over and over in my head as I sat in the backseat of Granma's green Oldsmobile station wagon, with my sister Ebony sandwiched between Mallory and me.

I am sure the drive only took about thirty minutes, but as an eight-year-old kid, it felt like forever—forever and a day as I waited to meet my father.

As we got closer to our destination, a range of emotions overcame me. My tummy felt as though it were tied and twisted into a thousand knots, trying to break free from the anxiety I was feeling. I couldn't quite understand all that was happening. I was nervous, excited, afraid, and curious at the same time. I thought perhaps God had decided to answer my prayers today.

I had heard a lot of things about my father from Granma. She shared stories about his countless run-ins with the law, his violence toward women, and how he was a known drug dealer on the streets. Deep down I knew this wasn't how it was supposed to be—my father was supposed to meet me, not the other way around.

But as Granma, Mallory, Ebony, and I walked toward a red and brown brick building, I was ready to finally meet my father.

Walking into the building as if I were entering a dark dungeon to meet with the devil, I felt a pounding in my chest, like the walls might start closing in around me. The smoke coming from the building reminded me of exactly where we were going. I looked up at the blanketed windows, hoping to see if I could spot my father, but the black bars across the glass blocked my view.

I faded back into reality when jailhouse security met us to guide us in, and suddenly I was in prison. Walking into a twilight zone, the lighting was dim, and the smell grew stronger as the air closed in on us. The loud sound of doors closing left us feeling as though we were prisoners, too. Met by a person standing behind metal dividers and a glass window, I wondered what it was like to be behind bars. The person behind the counter solidified the somber mood as he looked down on us, unsmiling. My every move was being watched. I was afraid to laugh, smile, or even ask questions.

My eight-year-old eyes scanned all four of the dingy walls, looking in every direction, hoping to lock eyes with my father. Of course, I had no idea what he looked like, but I still tried to seek him out hoping I'd run into someone who looked like me. Whenever I imagined us finally meeting, I pictured my father telling me I was beautiful and that he loved me. I had eagerly awaited his call to say, "I'm here. I can't wait to meet you." But it never came.

Now, as we stood to the side while Granma provided our birth certificates and social security cards to the lady behind the counter, I saw inmates dressed in all-white clothing walking around with their food trays. The food looked like pig slop—a messy, wet mix of various leftovers followed by a gross smell. That was enough for me to decide that prison life wasn't for me, not knowing at the time that this was reality for many Black men and women.

Despite my fear and anxiety, I tried to wait patiently. I could have burst from excitement. Things appeared to be going well, but just as we were about to walk through the metal detector, we were stopped.

"Wait one moment, ma'am," said one of the officers. I gasped at the sudden roadblock. He checked his papers while I continued to scan the lobby. Lost in a world of uniformity, I didn't hear the officer tell Granma that she forgot one of her forms of identification.

Before I could protest, she took our hands, turned us around, and led us out of the prison. I was inconsolable.

Disappointment, sadness, and anger flooded my body. I had been *this close* to meeting my father. All the questions I wanted to ask still lingered in my mind. We set up another day to come back, but my brain didn't stop swirling until then.

Weeks later, we returned and were finally able to go in. We went through the usual protocols, except this time we had to take off our shoes and put all our things in the lockers. The whole process felt dehumanizing, but that didn't matter at the time—I was ready to meet my dad.

I grew up watching *Cops, America's Most Wanted* and other shows and movies that often depicted prison as a scary, dark, and violent place for very bad people. Entering the prison, I wondered, *Is someone going to attack me? Am I safe? Would my father protect me? Will I have to talk to him through a hole, separated by a thick pane of glass? Can Daddy hug me, hold me, and pick me up? Will I only get to hear his voice through the jail phone, and not in real life?*

Turns out, my fears were unjustified. Finally making it through security, I realized jail was different from how television or movies depicted it. There wasn't major chaos, and I never witnessed big, angry Black men fighting or shouting. The only things that seemed consistent were the terrible food and dingy, stained off-white clothing.

Led by security, I entered the visitation area. To my surprise, the space was open, with lots of tables and chairs, and even a vending machine full of goodies. The walls in the room were dark white, like the walls in our school cafeteria. The long rectangular tables and black plastic chairs reminded me of the chairs we sometimes sat in during class, too. The atmosphere was open and monitored—we were constantly being watched. I saw men in white jumpsuits, gathered with friends and family.

Granma walked toward the tables and we followed, trying to figure out which man was our father. Was he tall or short? Skinny or fat? Seconds later, a tall, hulk-like man was before me. He was dark-skinned like Mallory, and had a big nose like me. He wore glasses and had a long braid coming from the back of his head—that was the style then. We shared his big, round brown eyes.

He held each of us as we fought for his attention. We all wanted to sit by Daddy and never let him go. As we chatted briefly, he went into his pocket and handed each of us a dollar bill.

"Go get ya selves something from the snack machine," he said.

We perked up, looking into Granma's eyes, hoping she'd say yes. She agreed, and we walked quickly over to the machine. This felt like heaven!

While the rest of my friends ate chocolate chip cookies, Lay's potato chips, and Lucky Charms, I was eating Wheaties, boiled brussels sprouts, and turkey burgers on a daily basis. Here was my chance to get whatever my heart desired, especially since a dollar would buy me at least two snacks. This dollar my father gave me was the greatest gift I had ever received—I was thinking this man was rich!

His action at the time made me feel extremely loved, but as I look back, I am somewhat ashamed that it only took one dollar for me to feel loved. To me, that dollar represented a kindness I'd gone without my whole eight years of life. He gave it to me purely because I was his daughter. Knowing that transformed him from an absent father to my greatest hero.

Meeting my father in person and seeing him laugh, feeling him hold me, and hearing him ask questions about my life like fathers did changed my perspective of him. He wasn't this bad guy that everyone painted him out to be—at least, I didn't think so at the time. I wasn't aware of all of the things my father had done.

I learned more about who he truly was through Mallory's anger.

When my older brother took his anger out on Ebony and me through countless chokeholds, Granma would refer to him as a coward—"a man who beats girls."

During Mallory's destructive rages Granma compared his violent behavior to our father's, but I didn't think she really meant it because my father's demeanor in the jail cell was different. He was cool, calm, and collected. I wondered if he was really as bad as Granma had painted him out to be.

"Okay, time's up. You have five more minutes, so start saying your goodbyes now!" shouted one of the guards.

Why couldn't time stand still while I basked in these last few moments with my Daddy? I didn't want the visit to end, I didn't want to leave, and I didn't want my dad to live there. I wondered if I'd ever see him again. If so, I hoped it was outside the prison walls and barbed-wire fences.

A Bitter Reality

A bittersweet journey home left me feeling conflicted in all kinds of ways. I was happy I had met him, sad to have left without him, and hopeful that someday he would come home so we could be a family again.

I dreamed up a gazillion things we were going to do together, like running around and playing in the backyard, going on bike rides, and going to get ice cream. I was so ready for him to be the father I wanted and dreamed for him to be. I thought about how cool it would be for he and Granma to come together like a dream team and care for us, and maybe things would be easier.

At home we returned to the basement where we usually stayed and to the routine of taking off our coats and hats and washing our hands. I walked into Granma's office area, excited and hopeful to share this blissful dream I had planned up.

"Granma?"

"Yes, my dear," she said softly.

"Can our dad come to live with us?"

"Oh, Imani," she squealed her nickname for me, laughing as if my request were outlandish, "where is he gonna stay?"

"In Daryl's room!" I exclaimed, referring to Granma's youngest son.

"Your father living here would not be a good idea," Granma said, referring to her role as a daycare provider.

But there's so much room here! I thought. My mind couldn't quite comprehend the dilemma, especially after witnessing with my own eyes that my father was a good man. I mean *come on*—he gave each of us a dollar.

I didn't know much about him, but I still wanted to believe my father was a good person. It just didn't feel good to know he was in jail.

"Why is he locked up anyways? He didn't try to kill anybody, did he?" I asked.

"No, he didn't, my dear," she replied.

Even as a little girl, I was intuitive, compassionate, and empathetic. I couldn't quite describe my actions as compassionate at the time, but I knew being confined in a small place could not be comfortable. This was my own reality, as my siblings and I were often confined in the basement with little connection to the outside world unless we were at church or school, or running errands with Granma.

Our small space became even more apparent when Granma tuned to the nightly news to catch *Sixty Minutes*. As annoying as it was to hear the clock tick and tock before the program started, I knew something important was going to be reported. These programs, along with the *Feed the Children* commercials, shed light on the cruel injustices of the world. Seeing other people locked up made me think of my father and wonder how he could survive such a place. I remember feeling a sting as I looked around that visitation room, seeing a room full of people whose family members were incarcerated.

I feared the fate of my father, and while I hoped he knew how much I cared about him and hoped for his freedom, I felt sure I would never see him again—although what felt like forever was actually four years. Until then, I clung to the only memory I had of him. He had generously handed me a dollar, and I never questioned where that dollar came from. I just eagerly slid my new crisp dollar bill into the vending machine, waiting for my taste of heaven in *my* father's house.

CHAPTER 2:

IN BETWEEN TWO EXTREMES

The doorbell rang. Mac-mena, our family social worker, stood in the doorway holding a light, buttery-brown baby in her arms. Just a year and a half prior, Mac-mena showed up to the same residence and placed my older brother and me in Granma's care. He was around three years old, and I was two. We were roughly two to three years older than this little baby by the time she arrived, leaving an imprint on my heart forever.

The baby screamed, her body rebelling against its very existence, forcing her to reconcile the trauma she had endured for the past six months while living on the streets with our mom. Her screams echoed throughout the home, which caused chaos, confusion, and disruption in our once peaceful environment. I couldn't quite piece together why she was so scared as she scanned her new surroundings. By the sound of her cries, you would have thought someone was trying to kill her.

In an effort to escape her screaming wrath, I sat in the corner and covered my ears, trying to avoid the uncontrollable sound in the distance.

Granma and Mac-mena made every attempt to calm her, but to no avail. My baby sister, Ebony, boomed into our lives, centering herself, and making it known that she was my fierce baby sister. From the moment Ebony appeared her voice was unshakable, leaving a permanent impression for the world to hear.

Even as a child, Ebony was a talker. She could talk your head off for hours and carry on a conversation better than most adults. She expected our full attention at all times, which forced us to engage with her until she decided it was our turn.

She was a bratty little sister who was annoying, bossy, and wanted things her way. Even though Ebony was small in stature, she was persistent, independent, and stubborn, easily wrapping both Mallory and me around her little finger.

Often, people confused me as the younger sister instead of Ebony because I had a quieter and shier demeanor. My Aunty Bernita, one of Granma's older daughters, described me as being "in between two extremes" because I was in the middle of two contrasting personalities.

While I was too afraid to make noise, Ebony and Mallory did not hold back. They were more confident and vocal about sharing their frustrations no matter the cost, while I often stood quiet, a wallflower.

Early on, I learned to appease others because I had seen that consequences came from not being "obedient." Adults in my life would make me feel bad via emotional abuse when I didn't obey others.

One evening, while Granma was styling our hair for annual picture day, Ebony did the unthinkable.

"I'm warning you, don't do it!" Granma urged after spending hours doing her hair. Ebony was the type of child who would do the opposite of what adults asked her to do, no matter the consequences. With each strand, Ebony continued taking out every braid and hair barrette, one by one, as Granma looked on.

And then Granma returned with a pair of scissors and began chopping off Ebony's hair.

"I told you, if you took out your hair, I would cut it all off," Granma scolded as Ebony wailed.

I stared in disbelief—in the blink of an eye, Ebony went from a head full of hair to an uneven afro.

While I was not the most excited about the old-school way Granma did my hair—big dookie braids and barrettes—I wasn't bold enough to take my hairstyle out even though I wanted to follow in Ebony's footsteps. When Granma made up her mind about something, she couldn't care less about what you thought. She would go to extremes when it came to parenting, with a just-do-as-I-say-without-question mentality, which often left us in the dark about things.

As a child, I wanted some sort of ownership and control over my life. I always felt like a visitor with no real place or things to call my own.

We lived in a three-story house with over four bedrooms, yet the basement became our room as we shared the space with her daycare children. Most days and evenings were spent in that basement while the rest of the house was mostly off limits, except during the holidays or wintertime. The basement was full of character, as it showcased our annual class pictures, nursery rhymes, and historical figures.

Mother Goose, Humpty Dumpty, and Jack and Jill nursery rhymes hung prominently against the walls, leaving little space for me and my siblings to contribute. Never having a space to call our own, I regularly dreamed about what it would mean and feel like getting to decorate my own space.

During the winter, I was especially thankful to sleep upstairs because it felt more like a home. To this day, I don't know why we were kept in the basement—but Granma had enough empathy to let us stay upstairs when it was really cold.

Our rooms were closer to Granma's then, and we were finally able to sleep on real beds instead of lying on plastic cots with just a sheet and my hands as improvised pillows. It felt like a treat to be able to sleep upstairs in Granma's children's rooms, with three fluffy white pillows at the top of the bed and the matching white quilt comforters keeping me warm.

I never questioned why things were the way they were. "Being grateful" was a value Granma had instilled in us very early.

As children, we were frequently reminded about Granma's good deed (and how incapable our parents were) through the praises of church members and people in her circle, who often told her that she was doing a good thing by taking care of us.

These adults made it clear she was doing us a favor, and this favor was held over our heads anytime we did something she didn't approve of. As a shy child who was sensitive to others' emotions and feelings, I attempted to keep the peace between my siblings because "one bad apple spoils the bunch."

If any one of us disobeyed, we all suffered. Like the scales of justice, I held the weight of my siblings' pain while also trying to maintain peace between them and Granma.

Even though Granma was strong-willed and independent, I sensed when she was overwhelmed because she would go upstairs for long periods of time, locking us in the basement without supervision.

Through the metal bars on the windows, I'd look toward the sun or bury my head in a book to distract myself from the sounds of my stomach growling. As the neighborhood kids ran up and down the street while we were caged in, I envied their laughter and freedom.

Spending long periods without food, water, or light, each time I heard a sound, I'd hope to finally hear the basement door twist open. Pushing on my stomach to remove the gas bubbles, I hoped the hunger pains would subside.

Sometimes it was too late by the time food came. The sharp aches in my stomach amplified so that it was too difficult to eat. I usually just handed my peanut butter and jelly sandwich over to Mallory.

I cried because I was famished, but I was in too much pain to eat anything.

Bonded by Trauma

During the weekends, our typical routine consisted of waking up at the crack of dawn to play together. Before doing so, Mallory would help me hang up my urine-dampened sheets on the heated pipes above us in hopes they would dry before Granma came downstairs. If my sheets weren't dry, then Granma would go outside, grab a branch off the tree, and beat me. Mallory was tall, so he was able to hang the sheets for me.

Energized and ready to go in the mornings, our imaginations transformed the basement around us. The white laminate floor quickly became an ice-skating rink where we slipped on our socks, gliding across the slick floor, pretending to skate. I would slip and slide, running away from my brother as he tried to catch me before I hit the base. I'd fall to the floor and yell, "Time out!"

It was all fun and games until it wasn't. We could easily go from playing together to fighting like cats and dogs. Mallory was a lot stronger than Ebony and me, and he gladly used his force against us by laying the smack down on us every chance he got.

"Can you smell what the rock is cooking?" he would chant before pushing us to the ground. To keep from crying, we laughed, made fun of each other, and did things to be funny.

One evening, Mallory, Ebony, and I were sitting in front of the television with our legs crossed on the floor. This was a typical pastime as Granma cleaned the kitchen. A commercial came on that proposed help for those dealing with bad breath. The timing was perfect, as we had just finished ragging on Ebony about her bad breath since she was always up in our faces. I don't remember the exact words that were said, but I remember hearing, "If you know someone with bad breath, please call 1-800-breathattack."

"Oh my gosh, did you hear that?" I exclaimed, shaking Mallory's shoulders and repeating what I had heard.

We busted out laughing, the type of laugh where your belly hurts. Ebony denied that the announcer had said it, but Mallory and I convinced her otherwise.

It became a perfect statement to blackmail her with. Anytime Ebony tried to protest or make fun of us, our comeback would be, "Yeah, yeah . . . shut up, before we call 1-800-breathattack on you!" Mallory and I often became a force against Ebony when she tried getting her way.

While these were silly moments, they were also crucial moments that helped us use laughter as an escape and an attempt to make our very unhappy situation more bearable.

We relied on each other for survival, confiding in and holding each other up when we needed it. My siblings were the ones who truly understood what was going on when no one else did.

Despite everything we went through, our experiences together sealed our lasting bond as we grew up. Granma was keen on instilling in us the importance of caring for each other. She taught us the golden rule, which was sometimes mentioned after an argument or fight: "Treat others the way you want to be treated." We were thick as thieves, and no one could take that away from us.

Thick as Thieves

Very early on, food was scarce. I was not always sure when my next meal would come, so I either rummaged through the garbage cans during morning breakfast at school, hoarded what I had, or stole when necessary. I was sneaky and knew how to be creative when it came to getting my needs met, even if it wasn't through the most sanitary of methods.

One afternoon, Mallory, Ebony, and I were outside playing when I suddenly became hungry. Because we could go long periods without eating, I would do everything to avoid feeling those hunger pains that were like a knife piercing my stomach. I conjured up a plan without confiding in my siblings. We were walking to the corner store on Blue Hill Avenue, a main commercial corridor, and with my little legs I went running across the street, avoiding the busy intersection. With pennies jingling in my pocket I opened the door, the hanging bell notifying the store owner that I was there. Standing in the aisle, I glared over at the Little Miss Debbie's Oatmeal Cream Pies, Peanut Butter Wafer Sticks, Starbursts, and Skittles.

One by one, I began stuffing my pockets and underwear. I walked toward the cash register and, leaning onto the ice cream freezer, I dug into my pockets and pulled out a mixture of dirty and shiny pennies that I had found on the ground.

"Excuse me, do you take pennies?" I asked, knowing damn well the items would cost more money than I had.

"No, sorry we don't," the store owner replied.

I bolted out of the store like a bat out of hell and ran home with my prizes, eagerly awaiting the chance to tease Mallory and Ebony with my goodies. I always got first dibs on the snacks but still shared them with my brother and sister.

From that day on, stealing came easily to me. I felt I couldn't stop stealing because I couldn't risk not knowing where my next meal would come from. I didn't want to feel hunger pains since they hurt, so I created a food pantry for myself. I had to think two steps ahead. My siblings were facing the same pains I was, and it was important for me to look out for them.

CHAPTER 3:

OVERSHADOWED

Most children grow up hearing from their parents or caregivers that they are special. I knew I was special, but for different reasons than one might expect.

On the first day of second grade, I stood outside my house watching a yellow school bus drive slowly down the street. With red and yellow flashing lights glaring down the street, a red and white stop sign slowly emerged from its side as it approached me. I was a little confused, as this was not the type of school bus I had seen Ebony ride. This one was much smaller, like a six-passenger van.

"You sure you sent the right bus?" I asked, hoping the driver had the wrong address, but deep down inside I knew what was going on. As the bus monitor opened the door for me, I was greeted with a smile and a helping hand to lift me up into the van.

First of all, I am not special! Why do I have to ride the special ED bus? I angrily questioned myself. *Why can't I walk to the bus stop like my other friends?* None of the regular kids rode the short SPED bus. That bus was for kids who needed special education classes.

I didn't need assistance to get to school; I just needed assistance in the classroom. Riding the small school bus every morning put a huge damper on my confidence, as it was no secret to the other students that I was a different type of special. Being escorted from one class to the next was painful because I caught heat from students who were in regular classroom settings in times of class transitions.

As my classmates and I were segregated on one side of the hallway walking, the other side of the hallway was filled with a long line of students hurling insults and laughter yelling, "You SPEDS!" as they pointed in our direction.

"Just ignore them," the teacher would say, but the magnitude of the bullying left stains of shame and worthlessness.

While the classroom offered some sense of safety, I couldn't help but notice that I still struggled despite being in smaller classes.

Being taken out of the classroom for speech therapy and counseling contributed to feeling hyper aware of my differences. It wasn't easy to grasp onto information—I needed constant repetition, redirection, and assurance that I was smart.

Communicating the challenges I faced in the classroom was difficult. I became frustrated if I didn't understand something, and then I completely shut down. I was often in a daze with a lot of worries on my mind. Finding comfort near the windows, I'd space out until the teacher called on me to answer a question I knew nothing about. I was at war with myself and got lost in self-doubt, criticism, and hopelessness.

Teachers often described me as friendly, cooperative, and compassionate, but also noted the following in my second-grade Individualized Education Plan (IEP) yearly evaluation: "Imani is a very smart girl who does not work up to her potential. She tends to be extremely lazy and needs to be encouraged to do her work." What teachers may not have known or cared to investigate is that I lived in an environment where I experienced neglect.

Many days, I came to school without having eaten breakfast. I looked forward to lunchtime because it was the only full meal I'd have for the day. I would wrap my arms around my tummy to quiet the gurgling sounds as the knots in my stomach grew tighter and tighter, like a rubber band waiting to pop.

To distract myself from the pain, I became fixated on the sound of the ticking clock, which soothed my ears because it meant that lunchtime was quickly approaching. As soon as the bell rang, I'd jump from my seat, racing to be the first person in line.

Rushing to the cafeteria, I gobbled my food down and stayed behind in the cafeteria until everyone had left so I could shuffle through the garbage can for my next snack or meal. If no one saw me, I could escape another insult, but this meant I was late to recess. I was willing to risk missing out if it meant that my hunger pains would subside.

Navigating these struggles while trying to learn made it challenging. While I dreamed of making it out of school one day and going to college, I was unsure of how I would since the education system did not feel like it was on my side.

No matter how hard I forced myself to work, learning became increasingly difficult over the years. I often felt overshadowed by the academic achievements of other students. I watched them win awards while I got recognized for minuscule things like perfect attendance. I barely had anything to show for the work I did except the bruised and broken crayons laying on my desk that I used to mindlessly doodle.

These bruised and broken crayons became a symbol of how I saw myself as a child. While I was considered neither traditionally special nor traditionally perfect, I tried my best in the midst of chaos. What I later learned is that broken crayons can still color even if they are overshadowed by all the perfect ones.

CHAPTER 4:

BURIED SECRET

In the dark of the night, I woke up to the abrupt sound of the flushing toilet. I was lying on the floor in Aunt Mozell's guest bedroom when a big dark shadow emerged in the doorway. As the shadow lurked closer, the streetlight outside the window beamed into his eyes, revealing who he was. His eyes met mine; it was my uncle.

Aunt Mozell was my Great Aunt on my mother's side, and we often went to her house to visit my older sister and other family members, or when Granma needed a break. Earlier in the evening, my uncle had been tossing my six-year-old body across Auntie's queen-size bed along with Mallory, who was eight, and Ebony, who was five. I had hurled out in laughter, wanting more and yelling, "Throw me again, throw me again!"

But in the blink of an eye everything seemed to change.

He hovered over me, and his body revealed my innocence; I wore my *Little Mermaid* nightgown and a Huggies pull-up diaper. The weight of his hands concealed my voice and he said, "Shh, don't say a word."

My body succumbed as if my soul was leaving my body. Weeping silently and repulsed by his sweat, I closed my eyes and wished this nightmare would hurry up and end. The sun began rising slowly, and the light swept over my face. I braced for an escape. I ran to the bathroom and scrubbed every inch of my body, wanting to rid myself of his invasion, but no matter how hard I scrubbed, I couldn't get rid of the stain. The layer of his violence was met with silence as I kept this buried secret hidden in the back of my memory for years, until the only brother I had shared this secret with Granma.

Mallory became my mouthpiece, and I was both angry and relieved that he revealed my truth. Granma acted quickly, pressing charges against my uncle, but I never had my day in court. The prosecutors felt I was too young to know exactly what had happened; this took away my ability to share my truth.

Experiencing sexual abuse at such a young age took away the little confidence I had about myself. Instead, I developed an aversion toward my body as if I wanted to betray it. Already feeling unwanted by my parents, this experience reaffirmed the hatred I had for myself. My once peaceful sleep now turned into daunting nights when I hid under the sheets to avoid seeing shadows.

Beneath the Surface

A few weeks later, I was told I would be seeing a counselor for several weeks to come. This was my first time meeting a counselor, and I was nervous. Typically, students were taken out of the classroom in the middle of a lesson if they were going to the principal's office or seeing a counselor. I was one of the students being pulled out to meet a counselor, and it felt embarrassing because kids picked up on things. Mrs. O'Connoley, one of the school administrators, allowed me to cling onto her arm, walking hand in hand through the hallways. She reassured me I was going to be in good hands.

Minutes later, a white woman with brown hair and a stocky but feminine build met us.

"Hello, my name is Lisa," she said, bending down toward me with her arm stretched out.

With my head down, I greeted her shyly. "My name is Imani." At the time, I thought my name was spelled and pronounced "Imani." Later I would learn this was not the case.

We started the sessions off slowly, and as each session passed, we dug deeper and deeper into that painful night. At the time it was difficult to understand why I was violated by my own uncle, but Lisa consistently reassured me it wasn't my fault, that I was only a kid.

The following week, I showed up to therapy and pre-cut construction paper waited for me on the table. The bright paper lured me into my seat, and I was eager to know what Lisa had prepared for me. As she pulled the box from under the table, Lisa shared, "This box is for you. I want you to use the construction paper to write out any feelings that come up and things you wish to say to your uncle."

I placed my feelings in the box one by one. A few sessions later, the box overflowed with thoughts about that night. During our last session, Lisa shared that we were going to bury the box.

I struggled with the idea of burying it because I didn't want anyone to find it. Burying it meant that I had to let it go, and I wasn't quite ready. My body still held the pain.

"We are going to bury this box deep so that no one finds it," Lisa stated. We walked behind the back of the school, and there was soft soil and a shallow hole already waiting, ready for us to dig. It helped that the weather was sunny and cool, making it perfect to be outside. The playground was empty. As birds swarmed the area, the chirping sounds kept me on my toes.

Before burying the box, Lisa and I cleared the hole so the box could sit perfectly in the dirt. Would everything go back to normal again as if nothing had happened to me? Would the big, scary monster in my dreams disappear and stop hurting me? Would my fear of the dark go away? Emotion after emotion could be felt through my tiny hands as I worked hard to let the box go, but then my hands froze. Lisa rubbed my back as tears streamed down my face and I held the box tightly.

After a few moments, Lisa began sharing words of encouragement, having me repeat after her, "You are loved, you are beautiful, and you are perfect." I said a few words of my own to finalize the moment and laid the box in its hole, throwing dirt on top of dirt until I could no longer see the box. Wiping the residue off my hands and onto my clothing felt like closure was finally taking place. Lisa and I embraced with a tight hug, and she reassured me that I was safe. I was going to be okay.

This was an important moment in my life because I was given the space to process my feelings around the abuse I had endured. I did not have all the language to express what I truly felt, but Lisa created space for me to see and know that I mattered. Buried underneath the scars, I somehow found the ability to find strength in laughter. I appreciated the sunlight even more—because the light that shined brightly on my face was the same light that hardened the soil, burying the big, dark shadow deep below the surface.

CHAPTER 5:

BLACK GIRL IN THE MIRROR

"Mirror, mirror on the wall, who's the fairest of them all?"

The television screen constantly displayed subconscious messages that led me to believe I was not beautiful or good enough, because I didn't see people who looked quite like me.

This led to a poor self-image mixed with self-hatred, which left me grasping to meet societal standards of beauty that were never within reach. I lived in a community where the people around looked like me, but everywhere else, I saw the "real" standard of beauty.

On television, all I saw were little white girls with blonde hair and blue eyes, and all the stores sold white baby dolls. This inadvertently told me that my beauty was despised.

Although Granma was pro-Black and intentional about hanging up powerful historical black images, like those of Parks, Hughes, and King, this did not stop me from viewing and perceiving myself through a distorted lens.

There was a dresser in the basement where I looked at my reflection in the mirror. My big brown eyes would scan back and forth across my tiny face, following the shadowy darkness I felt within. My reflection pierced me as I attempted to catch glimpses of my beauty. It seemed easier to zoom into the focal points of the immediate disdain I felt. I often heard words of encouragement from the church mothers. "Little girl, you are so beautiful; just look at you!" they would say, squeezing my hand as a reminder. But I could not reconcile their words with how I felt when I looked at myself in the mirror.

I heard that intimidating voice in my head again, saying, "Imani, if you only looked like those girls on TV, you would be pretty!" I could never pinpoint whether this voice was my nightmare or my own mind speaking to me. Instead of focusing on the positive qualities I saw within myself, my mind blocked those memories. It played back all the times I had counted the number of flaws and internal scars I saw on my ugly brown face.

In search of loving myself, I tried doing temporary things to boost my confidence. Most of the girls in my class had their ears pierced, probably from the time of their birth, but Ebony and I became the exception.

I was determined to get what I wanted, ripping pieces of stickers off my completed work and adding them onto my ear. Living with a caregiver who was close to sixty years older than us was a struggle. She was pretty conservative, following the Bible as closely as she could and stating scriptures like 1 Corinthians 3:16–17: "Do you not know that you are God's temple and that God's Spirit dwells in you? If anyone destroys God's temple, God will destroy him. For God's temple is holy, and you are that temple."

Earnest at heart, she was never quick to go back on her word. You knew not to ask again when she said, "No, I mean business," in her stern voice. She was intentional in what she did to make meaning out of the wisdom she shared. I couldn't always see it then, but I can appreciate it now.

Beauty Is in the Eye of the Beholder

Part of my path to understanding my inner beauty, worth, and value came from my Aunty Bernita. She was my dope cousin who lived in New York City and came to visit every so often. Even though she wasn't really my aunt, she allowed us to call her "Aunty" because my cousins called her that, and I believe she didn't want us to feel left out.

Aunty Bernita was the stereotypical aunt who didn't have her own children but treated every child she encountered with love. Not only was she nurturing, but she was also kind, witty, intellectual, and downright gorgeous. Aunty Bernita carried herself with class but could come up with jokes that had you laughing for minutes. My favorite part of Aunty Bernita was her generous nature. We were not allowed to chew gum at home, but with each visit I could count on Aunty Bernita to slide me a piece of her favorite sugarless Bubble Yum. It felt like I had won a prize!

Not only did I look forward to the gum, but I also looked forward to her presence because it was a reminder that I mattered. Because Mallory, Ebony, and I spent most of our time in the basement entertaining ourselves, there was always a sigh of relief when Bernita came to visit. During one of her visits, she and I stood in the mirror together as she showed me the trick of blowing bubbles. I thought she was a pro as she taught me how to curl the gum around my tongue and blow.

"You gotta do it like this," she would say as I blew until I got it right. During these times, we laughed, giggled, and tried a few times before the conversation shifted. We stared into each other's eyes through the mirror, as she pointed out the brown mole-like dot in her eye.

"This is my beauty mark, you see," she stated, as she pointed to the blemish in her eye.

"What is it?" I asked, in awe of what I saw.

"It's a mark of beauty, an attractive feature that many of us have," she shared. "It's rare because not many people have them in their eyes."

Then she pointed out that I had a beauty mark, just like hers, but mine was in the opposite eye. I looked closer in the mirror, perfectly concentrated on the black dot sitting near the back of my pupil, and I glimmered with a long smile, "Wow, I'm beautiful, just like Aunty."

She pulled me in closer and reminded me of the beauty I had within. As a little Black girl dusted with trauma, low self-esteem, and a learning disability, I felt as though Aunty Bernita's touch became the cloth that wiped away some of the negative perceptions I had of myself. Even though I struggled with believing that every aspect of myself was beautiful, sharing special moments with Aunty Bernita made it easier for me to look in the mirror. As if staring through a kaleidoscope, I grew in reassurance that the different patterns and elements of my natural beauty—even a stain in my eye—were proof of my value and worth.

Aunty Bernita's presence in my life continually showed me that the little Black girl in the mirror who often felt afraid and ashamed about who she was had remarkable features that went deep beyond her brown skin. They say that "beauty is in the eye of the beholder," and it turned out that a small, dark-brown speck in my eye led me to see and experience my beauty differently.

Little Black girl, you are worthy!

PART TWO:

2000-2002

CHAPTER 6:

THE ANTICIPATED ARRIVAL

For so long I felt imprisoned, trapped in a body I didn't create or ask to be in along with living in a locked basement isolated from the world as I watched children have a childhood I didn't get to fully experience. This was about to change, though, because at the tender age of ten my siblings and I were finally going to move in with my biological mother.

I don't remember all of the details, but during our last visit at Aunt Mozell's house, I remember looking at my mother and asking her, "How come Tiffani, my older sister, lives with you, and Mallory, Ebony, and I don't?"

She responded with a promise: "I am going to work hard to get you all back."

I believed her. I assumed things would be different because my mother was a lot younger than Granma, which meant she could play, spend time with us, and do mother-daughter activities. We would no longer have to view the world from the dark basement as my siblings and I watched kids screaming, laughing, and riding their bikes up and down the street. Most importantly, I was looking forward to being held and nurtured by my mother, something I rarely received.

Sitting at the round, colorful plastic table like they had in the '90s, Ebony, Mallory, and I sat debating whether or not *Teenage Mutant Ninja Turtles* was better than *Power Rangers* when we were suddenly interrupted. The mood in the room felt different than usual, somber. I didn't hear *Sixty Minutes* playing in the background or hear the water in the kitchen running as Granma washed dishes while we ate like usual.

She hovered over us, trying to pull our attention from the debate. This evening, Granma informed us that my mother was granted temporary custody of us, which meant we would be leaving soon. The fairy tale I dreamed of for ten years was finally becoming a reality! What I looked forward to the most was finally being able to rest my head in my mom's arms as I lay on her chest while her heartbeat traveled to my eardrums.

Along with this came with so many compounding emotions. Thoughts and feelings soared through my brain as I wondered how Granma truly felt about us leaving. As a child who aimed to please adults, I wondered whether she was happy or sad? Did she think we didn't want to live there, or that we were ungrateful? Would she still be in our lives and come visit us? I was unsure and didn't know how to ask her, feeling somewhat guilty about how happy I was over this massive change. I knew we would at least be giving her a break, since she was about seventy-seven at this time.

Granma dropped us off at the light blue house on the corner of West Selden Street on a hot, sunny summer day. This place was not unfamiliar—it was the same place where I had been sexually violated four years prior.

At the time, my excitement for living with my mom outweighed the numbness I experienced from memories of my abuses as my body kept a score. Tempered by memories as flashbacks flooded through my mind, I still suffered from nightly nightmares, hoping they would finally stop because my mom could be there to protect me. The day I fantasized about my entire life was finally here.

Anxiously awaiting my mother's arrival, we were greeted by Aunt Mozell, who informed us that my mother was not home from work yet. We were all a bit disappointed, hoping she would be the first person to greet us with hugs and kisses; this was not the case.

Each of us carried a black trash bag full of our belongings and maneuvered them up the stairs. Quickly after, Ebony, Mallory and I eagerly began exploring our new place, googly eyes and all. We knew not to go into Tiffany's room because a few weeks prior we got caught stealing her stuffed animals out of her bedroom; she wasn't too happy with us.

Right next to Tiffany's bedroom was the bathroom, then the linen closet, and then the room belonging to Freeman— Aunt Mozell's longtime friend. This left three other rooms, and I was excited about the possibility of having my own. Then I learned Ebony and I would be sharing space in the converted living room while Mallory stayed in the coolest room of all: the indoor porch.

As we began settling in, I heard a key being placed in the hard wooden door as it unclicked. With reckless abandon we stopped unpacking and ran to the top of the staircase, anxiously waiting to see our mother's face.

This wasn't the first time I saw my mother, but it was my first time believing that everything was finally okay.

Her face illuminated the dark staircase. Walking up the stairs, all I saw was the bright glow on her dark-skinned face and her excitement at seeing us. Even though she was my mother, we didn't know how to greet her. Understanding our own confusion as to what to call her, she introduced herself as "Lael" and told us we could call her Ms. Lael if we didn't feel comfortable calling her "Mom."

While the immediate pressure of not having to call her mom was a relief in the moment, calling my mother "Ms. Lael" felt weird, but I went with it. It didn't take too long to settle in and unpack our belongings, but there were so many changes happening at once, including the drastic change in the spelling and meaning of my own name.

For the first ten years of my life, I was known to myself, my peers, church members, and family as Imani, which means "faith" in Swahili and is the seventh principle of Kwanzaa.

"That is not how you spell your name," my mother quickly interjected while I spelled my name one day. Confused, I wasn't sure what was going on. She shared with me that the name on my birth certificate was actually spelled A-M-N-O-N-I and not I-M-A-N-I. From that moment on, I bore shame around my name because my mother admittedly told me she didn't know how to correctly spell my name—she insinuated during one of our later encounters that it was because of the amount of drugs she was on when she had me.

Making me correct my name was a huge disappointment because I loved what "Imani" embodied, along with the ease of pronouncing it. I remember feeling special around Kwanzaa. It embodied a rich essence of Blackness and history that most people knew when I said what Imani stood for. I felt special knowing my name had significance. It was also a hard transition as it was easier to spell and pronounce "Imani" versus "Amnoni."

Changing my name felt as if my entire identity was stripped away, causing me to spend endless amounts of time correcting myself and others on a name I disliked. I grew more and more upset with my mother for coming into my life ten years late and correcting the way my name was once spelled. To escape embarrassment and bullying from students, I'd rush to be the first one in class so I could inform the teacher how to pronounce my name, so they could stop butchering it during attendance. Sometimes it worked, and other times it didn't.

Bearing the Weight of my Father's Sins

My name change soon became the least of my worries. The connection between me and my mom turned out to be not at all what I assumed. Like quicksand suddenly losing its strength and support, the honeymoon phase faded pretty quickly. Comparisons between me and my father were soon made, and she would often make comments about how ugly and horrible of a person he was and in the same sentence tell me I looked just like him.

I began to feel as though I was paying for the crimes my father committed against my mother. She often shared about the many times he tried to kill her, leaving me riddled with guilt that the person who helped create me also tried to kill me when he pushed her down the stairs while pregnant with me.

«He hit me the most when I was pregnant with you," my mother told me, "and he left me for dead when he beat me with a machete." She pointed to the scar across her forehead.

Feeling bad for the life she experienced, I often kept quiet about the things that happened to us, talking in private with Mallory and Ebony for comfort instead. The pattern became clear: Even though she was clean, sober, and attended Alcoholics Anonymous (AA) and Narcotics Anonymous

(NA) on a regular basis, my mother's care often felt abusive and neglectful.

As children who experienced food and water withholdings, I'd often snuck into the bathroom to quench my thirst. One evening during one of my mother's NA meetings, I was extremely thirsty, ready to swallow an entire ocean when I asked my mother if I could have something to drink. She said no, without an explanation. I felt like I was going to die trying to figure out how to get something to drink, but I quickly conjured up a plan knowing my mother was going to be sharing her testimony with the NA folks pretty soon.

"Hi, my name is Lael, and I'm an addict" is the phrase often used in these meetings.

I acted as if I needed to use the bathroom, walking slowly toward the kitchen where I was met by a group of ladies "cheffing it up." As my big brown eyes met theirs like a sad, lost puppy, I asked if I could have some water.

"Sure baby," one lady insisted as she offered a choice between fruit punch Kool-Aid and water. I chose the sugar instead, quickly gulping it down and running back to my seat before my mother would notice. Bragging to Mallory and Ebony that I got something to drink was a huge mistake; instead of being the loyal siblings they were supposed to be, they snitched on me in a heartbeat.

During the car ride home, my mother sat in the passenger seat and her friend drove us back to the house. My mother turned around, looked me in the face, and told she was going to "beat my ass" when we got to the house. Trembling inside, trying to gather a plan of how I was going to escape this beating, I realized saying "sorry" wasn't enough. Taking a deep breath, I thought about what I heard my peers were doing. They would put on extra underwear to help with padding.

Because I knew my mother was going to beat me "butterball naked" as she directed, I got undressed as soon as I got home; my plan was to put on extra underwear and throw tissue in there for extra padding, but I panicked.

Like a circus, my siblings gathered around and watched. My mother made sure to make a mockery out of me so her other children knew "what not to do," bragging about how I was the first child she would beat. It seemed as though she marveled in violence, laughing it off, and at that moment I no longer felt safe.

This wasn't the first or last beating I experienced from my mother, and each time the whoopings felt more intense as deeper welts appeared on my body and the internal scars continued to form.

My mother spent a lot of time working, so Mallory, Ebony, and I spent a lot of time together. When she wasn't around, I felt like I could finally breathe. When she was around, the environment felt tense and miserable, as if I was walking on a tightrope.

I struggled to fall asleep because I feared hearing my mother's footsteps in the night, not knowing if she was going to the bathroom or if she was going to wake me up for a beating. My nightmares increased and became more vivid. I began to see things; I'd wake up in the middle of the night thinking I saw a large man sitting in the golden-brown chair, only to wake up the next morning to a pile of clothing.

Too scared to move and too scared not to, I'd sneak into Ebony's bed at night, returning to mine before the sun rose so I wouldn't get in trouble. Ebony and I connected in this way because she was also the target of my mother's abuse, while Mallory had to watch it. It caused some friction between us, as we girls went from experiencing similar abuses to feeling as though Mallory was our mother's special child. Even if we all did something together, Ebony and I were punished while my mother treated Mallory to special desserts right in front of us. It caused some jealousy, but when my mother wasn't around the three of us came back together like the pack we were.

And while there were some happy moments—like our mother taking us to Chez-Vous, a local roller skate joint, on the weekends, or taking us on bike rides around the neighborhood, and even taking time from work to rush home and make sure I was safe when she learned my uncle who violated me returned to the house—it didn't make up for the harm she continued to create.

Deep down inside, I was disappointed. Not having the mother I waited for every year at the mother-daughter brunch left a gaping hole and more reasons not to trust. I felt misunderstood by her when she mistook my tears and sensitivity for being weak, often referring to me as a chicken instead of seeing me as traumatized.

I thought she would be happy to have her kids back in her life, but I wasn't so sure—she took more interest in the lovers she was with than she did in spending quality time with us.

The truth is I really wanted to spend time with her, but I was scared to be around her because she was so unpredictable. The dream of having a loving and caring mom quickly disappeared right before my eyes, and the promise of never giving us up again was slowly deteriorating.

CHAPTER 7:

THE LAST GOODBYE

Like so many other events in my life, once again everything was changing at such a rapid rate. I thought it was all a dream.

"Amnoni, stop what you're doing, and please come with me," one of the staff members shouted entering the gym, motioning for me to follow him off the basketball court away from my friends.

Ah man, what did I do? I thought. As we walked down the hall, my eyes followed his every move, wondering what was happening. He led me into one of the main conference rooms where students rarely went. I couldn't help but wonder if I was in trouble since that had been the norm lately. Instead, I walked into a situation that forever changed my life. My social worker, Ms. Comfort, who was standing in the room, met me along with Ebony and Mallory. Usually Ms. Comfort had a smile on her face, but not today. The room felt tense as Mallory and Ebony stood silently.

"What's going on?" I asked. "Did something happen to Mom, Tiffany, or Aunty?"

"I'm sorry, but I'm not going to be able to bring you all back to your mom's house tonight," Ms. Comfort replied in her Nigerian accent. Standing in silence and fidgeting with my fingers, I knew what this meant, but it didn't make sense.

"I thought our mom was going to wait until after Mallory and I graduated from summer school before she let us go. This can't be right."

When we first moved in two years prior, one of the first things I asked my mom when we returned to her custody was whether or not she was going to give us up again. She promised we would stay with her. Now here we were two years later, driving to the Department of Children and Families after hours to pick up our belongings.

"Here, you all get two duffle bags each," Ms. Comfort said as she handed us the black bags with "USA" written on the side. So many emotions went through my mind at once. I didn't know what to do. I was embarrassed and filled with shame that I hadn't behaved well enough to stay with my mom. I thought back to all the things I could've done to prevent this. Events started popping into my head as I thought about everything I had done wrong.

"Are we going back to Granma's house?" one of us asked.

"Unfortunately not."

I couldn't believe it. «Does Granma not want us anymore? I thought she said we could come back to her house if we were ever taken away."

"Sadly, Granma is too old now," Ms. Comfort said.

I continued to wonder who else would take us as one of my siblings went down the list asking about other family members.

"What about Linda and Kenny? Can they take us?" Linda and Kenny, Granma's son and daughter-in-law, often cared for us on the weekends.

"Unfortunately not; they already have five children. But don't worry, you all will stay in a safe place."

Rejected yet again. No one showed up at the DCF to claim us. How could it be so difficult for a family to take us in when there were only three of us and an entire flock of families around the United States? Was anyone even advocating for us, or were we labeled as "throw-away kids?"

Broken Promises

"There's never a reason to lie" was one of my mom's famous mantras she shared with us whenever she caught us in a lie, but this time the lie we told cost us our stability.

Gathered in the kitchen, my siblings and I stood as if on trial while my mom opened the freezer and pulled out a roll of cookie dough.

Here we go again, I thought. My mom seemed to look for things to be unhappy with us about. Holding the roll of frozen Pillsbury cookie dough in her hand, she yelled out, "Who ate some of my cookie dough?" as her piercing eyes stretched across our faces.

"I didn't!" I quickly responded, even though I was one of the culprits. I just didn't want to get in trouble.

Mallory, Ebony, and I stood there anxiously awaiting my mom's verdict, which either meant we were going to get a beating or my mother would angrily shut herself in her bedroom, giving us the silent treatment until she was ready, which could last for hours.

Walking away, I felt her frustration move through her feet as her slippers dragged heavily down the hallway while she screamed and yelled about how much she couldn't take care of us anymore: "I'm giving you all up; I no longer want to hurt you anymore!"

I wasn't sure whether she was referring to the cumulative abuse we had endured or last night's incident—when she accidently hit Ebony in the eye with the belt buckle while beating her. Despite all of this, "There is never a reason to lie" kept replaying in my head. My mother had promised she would never let us be taken away from her again. My mom could say some hurtful things when she was angry, so I believed the words she screamed now were more of the same.

This time she was serious, though. As I begged for her to keep us, she compromised: Since Mallory and I were both in summer school at the time, we agreed that giving us up right as the summer was ending wouldn't be a good idea. But she lied. We were scooped up without our belongings, never getting to say our last goodbye to my mother, older sister, Aunt Mozell, or other family members.

Fragmented Pact

As we gathered our bags and placed them in the trunk of Ms. Comfort's car, my stomach felt the weight of the experience crumbling on top of me. It felt as though someone was kicking me and forcing me to stay quiet as my throat quivered, a cry attempting to come out. During the entire car ride, a series of questions ran through my mind. *Where are we going? Who are we going to stay with?*

Soon thereafter we arrived in an area that looked somewhat familiar, as Boston was small. This was one of the routes our after-school bus driver, Tony, took to bring one of the students home from the after-school program. After some twists and turns down several streets, we arrived.

"Okay, we are here. Are you ready?" Ms. Comfort asked.

I'm sure we said something snarky—making jokes was one of the ways we dealt with the pain. I felt like I was just in a scene of the movie *Taken* where I was snatched up by some strangers and brought to an undisclosed location with little information about what was going on. I looked toward the evening sun as the cool summer sky was slowly setting.1 My stomach began to rumble like it usually did when I was in an unknown situation. As I sat beside my siblings, I could feel their unease, too. I didn't want to be here; I wanted to go back home. I wondered what was in there. Would there be other kids? Would the foster mother be nice? These thoughts surrounded me as I peeked out the car window.

Slowly stepping out of the car, we walked up to the porch and were greeted by our new foster mother, who was leaning on her silver cane for support. I wasn't impressed. She was old, perhaps in her eighties, with a salt-and-pepper bun and charcoal-like skin.

"Hello, my name is Mrs. Alabama. It's nice to meet you. Come inside." Her southern voice sounded raspy yet loud.

Stepping inside her house, the smell of mothballs almost instantly knocked me to the ground. I hated the smell of mothballs because the sharp paint-like odor stained your senses: It was hard to ignore. Standing in her dining room a few feet away from her kitchen, my mind couldn't stop racing. I tried to understand why we were there. Standing quietly together, we listened to Ms. Comfort share with Mrs. Alabama about who we were. I just wanted to get this meeting over with so I could be with my siblings. A few moments later, we learned that Ms. Comfort was dropping Mallory and me off but Ebony was going somewhere else. The burning sensation I experienced within my stomach felt like heartburn on steroids.

The ache moved from my stomach to my chest. I was shocked, angry, and powerless. How was I going to be able to sleep at night knowing my baby sister wasn't by my side? We had never been apart from each other for a long period of time, besides the two times our mom called DSS to provide respite because of Ebony's behavior.

This took me back to the long, dark nights I spent alone in my bedroom, struggling to sleep because Ebony wasn't there next to me. She was the protector of the night. Even though I knew her scrawny body couldn't do much, her presence provided relief.

No, she needs to be here with us, I thought as I pulled Ebony closer. I wanted to make a statement that this wasn't going to be easy, but it was too late. The nightmare had set in, and there was nothing I could do. Trying to buy more time with Ebony, I held her tightly in my arms and wondered if we were ever going to be okay.

Shortly after, as dusk set in, the rays of the sun cued that it was time for Ebony to go. Ms. Comfort needed to bring Ebony to her new placement, but all I wanted to do was hold Ebony tighter. I wanted to go with her. I didn't want to leave her because we took care of each other. How were we going to be able to do that if she wasn't here with us?

We followed her out to the car. Mallory walked behind me. We stood on the sidewalk, waving to Ebony as she sat in the backseat, looking back at us with her gloomy eyes as Ms. Comfort slowly drove away. While I was angry my mom gave us up, I was too angry to care about going home. I cared more about staying with my siblings, but the system wouldn't even give us the decency to say our proper goodbyes to each other, leaving our once tightly glued pack fragmented.

A New Normal

The next morning felt like a blur. I was discombobulated, experiencing déjà-vu. The layout of the basement reminded me of my Aunty Linda's house where my cousins, siblings, and I used to play. The pull-out couch Mallory and I slept on reminded me of the sweet honey smell of Cap'n Crunch pieces stuck between the couch, but nothing about being here felt sweet. The aroma of mothballs kept me up; I tossed and turned most of the night. I was in a new space. The bed wasn't my own. I woke up next to Mallory in the extreme darkness instead of Ebony. Dang—Ebony was *missing*.

Life didn't feel the same and I wanted her back. Sitting at the table eating white toast with grape jelly and eggs just didn't feel the same. The dynamic trio had lost the backbone of our sibling group, and although I was thankful I could stay with Mallory, he couldn't take my sister's place. We felt her absence everywhere. She was nowhere in sight, and I could no longer say "good morning" to her. I wondered what she was doing, if she liked where she was staying, if she would be with other people. I had so many questions, but no answers.

Later that morning, Mrs. Alabama fixed us bologna and cheese sandwiches on Wonder Bread with Miracle Whip. While I enjoyed bologna sandwiches, I didn't like cheese, white bread, or Miracle Whip because it made the sandwich too soggy. But I gave her no troubles and ate it. Soon after, she let us walk to the park. Although the park was a short distance away, the loneliness made walking a struggle.

The park used to be a fun place where I could get lost and indulge, but this day was different. I struggled watching kids play without a care in the world as their friends and family chased them through the park maze. I sat on the swings watching, dragging my feet as though the weight of the world was crumbling onto my shoulders. As days passed by, it felt a little easier to play because Mallory and I quickly made friends with the other kids on the street.

When we weren't spending time playing in the streets, we accompanied Mrs. Alabama to run her weekend errands. One morning, the heat was blazing. Mallory and I ran to her 1960s yellow Lincoln as she walked slowly behind us, assisted by her cane. As we arrived at the back door, about to open it, we were met by her loud, raspy voice.

"Wait! What y'all think y'all doing?" she squealed, giving us the Black Mama look with one hand on her hip and the other rested on her cane.

"Come ova here and help me close my door."

I was confused. *How come we gotta help her open her door? Yo, slave days are ova,* I thought. Then Mallory and I both looked down and saw why. As she sat in the car, the door lowered toward the ground.

"It broke!" she hollered.

In order to close her door, Mallory and I had to bend down to pick up her door while she sat comfortably in the car. Trying not to bust out in laughter, both Mallory and I looked at each other and it just came out.

"What ch'all laughing at?" she asked.

Mallory and I could not contain our laughter and picked up her door at the same time.

Each time she had to run an errand, we had to repeat this task. I was twelve, and he was thirteen. I was low-key resentful that we had to help her, but it was important for me to keep my mouth shut so I didn't cause any trouble and risk being kicked out.

Instead, we treasured this experience as an inside joke. Given that we were placed under emergency care with Mrs. Alabama, there was no telling how long we would stay or how long this would go on, which made it difficult to emotionally connect with her. We ended up staying with her through the summer.

The Translucent Interview

What I enjoyed most during the summers was riding the Massachusetts Bay Transportation Authority (MBTA) trains around the city, exploring through a bird's-eye view with lots of different people around. Staring outside the window from my seat, I loved following the trees and the differently colored cars, feeling the speed of the train rumble under my butt as it sped through the darkness of the underground tunnel.

I sometimes loved the mystery that darkness brought, but today's darkness felt a bit different. Accompanied by Ms. Comfort, Mallory, Ebony, and I packed on the orange line train wondering if we were there yet. I spotted the "State Street" train stop above the train doors, noticing we were seven stops away from our destination. My heart beat faster, matching the rhythm of the train. It had been a few weeks since we had been separated from each other, and we were heading to the Department of Social Services for a meeting.

When we arrived, we entered a room with two social workers. When we sat down, they told us to look to the left. Following their fingers, I couldn't see anything but a mirror.

"We just want to let you know that there is a group of people back there listening to what you are saying. Even if you can't see them, they can see you," they told us.

I concentrated on the glossy mirror, trying to figure out how they could see me, but I couldn't see them. The interview felt as though it lasted a whole day with the list of questions becoming more and more intense.

"Counting on your fingers, can you tell us how many times your mom hit you?" they asked.

"I don't know," I said. "Too many to count."

"Did she hit you with an open, closed fist, or belt?"

"All three," I responded.

Many of the questions forced me to recall the experience, detail by detail.

One thing about my mother is that her abuse was not hidden behind closed doors. In public it was more intense because the people around her rarely questioned or said anything when she threatened us. She would whip us and then encourage us to tell our teachers or any authority figure for that matter.

"You can pick up the phone and call 9-1-1 if you want to; they can't save you," she would say.

One time she beat Ebony with a ruler in front of her elementary school teacher during an open house while I watched in terror. She seemed to care little about the consequences that came with her actions, even getting on the phone with her friends and bragging about how she just "beat my ass."

This was a struggle to deal with because I wanted badly for someone to come to my rescue so I could escape her wrath, but I usually shrank in fear.

During one of the interviews, I remember recalling an incident when I believed my mother had almost killed me. To share the intimate details around what had happened was easier to do since I'd recently shared it with Ms. Cerci, the executive director of Linden Park.

The evidence of abuse had been glaring in Ms. Cerci's face as she greeted me with a hug, and then quickly pulled away and looking at my neck, she had asked, "What is that ring around your neck, sweetie?"

Honestly, I couldn't wait to tell her even though part of me was afraid.

"My mom choked me," I muttered.

Ms. Cerci's eyes widened, caught off guard by my answer.

As I recounted my story, she looked at me in disbelief. There were so many emotions, and I was trying to process and understand what happened. I had been ashamed to share that my own mother could have even thought to hurt me in this way.

I was outside running up and down the street with my brother and sister. As we ran, my mother yelled from up above, "Mani," my nickname, in a harsh tone telling me to come upstairs. Quickly running upstairs, even skipping some steps along the way, I thought I'd only be there for a quick second. A quick turn of events led to a bad nightmare. What I thought would be a quick interaction turned into something I never anticipated.

"Clean out this goddamn tub," she yelled as she pointed to the light ring around the tub.

Is this a joke? I wondered whether it really wasn't a joke, because my mother would wake us out of our sleep just to wash the one fork, knife, and spoon that lay peacefully in the sink. I asked no questions and began scrubbing. When she perceived I hadn't used enough elbow grease, her obsessive compulsiveness left her enraged. She slammed my head into the metal radiator, threw me into the tub, and then dragged me into the bedroom where the weight of her hands clenched around my neck. My jaw locked as if I were in handcuffs.

"I . . . can't . . . breathe . . . I . . . can't . . . breathe," I gasped, trying to squirm away from her. But I wasn't strong enough.

The anger in her eyes fixed on mine as if she were looking at my father. After what felt like forever, my mother finally let go of my neck.

"Go get your damn asthma pump," she yelled, as if I was the cause of her anger.

It was as if this was all a villainous plan. I wondered why I deserved this. Staring into the social worker's eyes and sharing this incident felt like a bitter betrayal. It felt like the people sitting behind the mirrored window, listening to every detail of my life story, were pondering about who could do this to their own child.

The Decision

Standing outside the courtroom waiting for my mother to make her appearance felt like forever and a day, but this meant I got to spend more time with Ebony.

As we awaited our fate, I wondered if life would ever be the same again.

Mallory, Ebony, and I paced up and down the hall anxiously waiting for her. Looking over the railing, all I could see was a sea of people dressed in business attire. My eyes scanned below looking for my mom as though we were playing a game of "Where's Waldo."

After hours of waiting, we learned my mother was a no-show. It seemed her absence had made the final decision.

Soon after, our social worker walked out of the courtroom bearing news that The Department of Children and Families was taking permanent custody of us, as though in winning the case they were cashing in on a major prize.

Later, my mom would claim she didn't have room to take us all in and that she was pregnant again, but at the time, all I could do was blame myself. Maybe if I hadn't written that letter about her abuse, she would have shown up.

CHAPTER 8:

A COLD SUMMER

A Bitter Reality

Learning how to navigate the foster care system is like learning how to ride a bike for the first time without training wheels. As a twelve-year-old, I was not handed a "Welcome to Foster Care" pamphlet outlining the dos and don'ts of how to succeed in foster care.

Instead, I was handed two black duffle bags with "USA" laminated across the sides, sealing my new identity as a ward of Massachusetts state. My mother had permanently lost her parental rights. It frustrated me not knowing all the details about why I was in foster care, and at the same time, I felt like I could breathe a little better because my new home would hopefully protect me.

The sun was blazing down onto my cheeks on the hot summer evening as my eyes followed the clouds in the sky leading my brother and me to our new home. Slowly opening the back door to my new social worker Mr. Issaic's (Issaic we called him) green Chevy, I closed the door behind me and stared at the baby blue house right in front of me.

"You are right around the corner from your Aunt Linda." Issaic mentioned it to help ease our nervousness. Knowing she was closer to us in proximity made the feelings about not being able to live with relatives all too real. At the time,

Granma was too old to care for us, too many of our family members had criminal records, and those who were qualified to care for us did not step up.

Issaic could see the sadness in my eyes as he looked at me and said, "You are safe."

I clung to my duffle bags. We walked up the red brick stairs to the double-door entrances. The left door led to the upstairs of my foster mother's house and the right door led to downstairs, where Mallory would soon live with the other foster mother. They were sisters who co-owned the house together.

Shortly after ringing the bell, the door opened and I was greeted by my new foster sister, who welcomed us in.

"Hi, my name is Mika," she said softly, grabbing one of my duffle bags out of my hands and helping me up the blue carpeted stairs. As if they had been preparing for my arrival, Febreze wafted through the house.

"Hi, my name is Ms. Mabel, but you can call me Auntie Mabel if you would like; my nieces and nephews call me that."

My eyes lit up, surprised to be invited so quickly into the family. Slumped over her walker, Aunt Mabel's wheels glided through the carpet as she led us to the living room. The living room had so much color—from the light blue wallpaper to the cloud-like couches and the blue carpet to match—I felt as if I was in the clouds for a moment. After sharing quick introductions, Mika brought me to our bedroom in the back of the house and toppled my things onto the top bunk. Soon after, Aunt Mabel sent us to the pizza joint down the street to pick up dinner. It didn't take long for me to feel comfortable and settle in, but just as the day turned into nighttime, the reality of being a foster kid quickly seeped in.

The next morning I awoke to a nightmare: a bed full of urine. Feeling soggy, wet, and frozen in the middle of the bed, I couldn't help but think back to the moment my mom threatened to beat me, insisting I was too old to wet the bed.

At ten years old she knocked the fear into me. Not understanding what had led to the bedwetting, I imagined that maybe the nightmares I had during the night paralyzed my body. I just hoped it hadn't seeped through to the bottom bunk where Mika slept—can you imagine waking up to warm pee on your face? As I prepared to leave for school, I walked by the pantry and saw an orange juice Guzzler lying alone in the closet. I swiped it up, put it in my bag, and left for school.

When I returned home that afternoon, Aunt Mabel asked if I had taken the juice that was in the closet. I lied and said no. The next morning, I noticed a white chain around the fridge with a master lock. The deep freezer and pantry were also locked. I felt like an animal in the wild, hunting for food that didn't exist. I blamed myself rather than say anything because I learned very early that food was not a basic right but had to be earned.

I've struggled with eating and body-image issues because the very adults in my life who were supposed to provide for my basic needs withheld from me instead. All of this led me to begin stealing. I wonder, if my foster mother had known how food was a trauma trigger for me, would she have still placed these locks on the fridge and pantry? No child should ever experience the feeling of hunger pains. No child should ever have to go to sleep hungry, wondering where the next meal will come from.

Soon after this happened, I learned that food wasn't the only uphill battle I would face. I would soon be the pendulum that swung between my new foster mother and my biological mother, and it was a place I didn't want to be.

Trapped between Two Worlds

After our removal, they granted my mother supervised visits with us. On a weekly basis, our social worker picked us up and brought us to The Department of Children and Families for our family visits.

Because Ebony didn't live with us, this was our opportunity to visit with her, too. At the time I felt conflicted about seeing my mom because I blamed myself for telling the courts how afraid I had been, which led to the supervised visits.

Often, Ebony, Mallory, and I would arrive at the visitation room before my mom. The three of us could talk a little trash because my mom's demeanor brought out my anxiety. It didn't make it easier that the room felt dark and cold. The walls were blank and dingy, and I sometimes played with the broken toys around me to help with the awkwardness. Not sure if I should hug my mom, I would walk to her to give a faint hug and barely squeeze her; she would hug me back.

The room always felt tense when she walked in and the laughs and giggles we shared before she arrived immediately stopped; you could hear a pin drop. As we all gathered by the round table, I would always sit next to Ebony for comfort.

Not long after her arrival, my mother would shout, "Oh, who did your hair like that?"

"My foster mother," I would say softly.

"Ew, why did she do that to your hair?"

Sitting in silence biting at my fingernails to soothe my nerves, my mom took out each braid without a care whether

I would get in trouble or not. Even though I never liked the fat, plaited braids in my hair, I wanted to keep them so as not to disturb the peace.

My mother seemingly never cared. She always took each braid out as she spewed negative comments about Aunt Mabel. Then I'd get home and get yelled at for not standing up to my mother and siding with Aunt Mabel, all the while feeling powerless.

"Your mammy always has something negative to say. If she wanted you, she would've had you," she would say.

If it wasn't my hair, it was the type of clothing Aunt Mabel dressed me in. I became the butt of the joke each week, and I already hated sitting in that dingy visitation room because my mom made things worse for me at the house.

To make matters worse, the one day I looked forward to, Sunday, was taken away. Aunt Mabel wanting to attend church as a family negated the experience and connection I had with the church I attended prior to living with Aunt Mabel. The church experience with Aunt Mabel was night and day from mine—her church was a different denomination, and it was not the church I was accustomed to for the last twelve years.

Growing up in the African Methodist Church, which was historically Black, I was surrounded by a congregation of people who valued the importance of community service within the church and around the community.

At the time, I was not aware of the pivotal role it played in my life until it was stripped away from me. Not only was I involved in the youth choir, but I was also a part of The Young People's Division where I participated in community service efforts, evangelism, and weekly Bible Study.

The church is where I felt some sense of normalcy and safety, given that some of my family members attended the church such as Granma, my Aunty Linda, and cousins. My weekend routines suddenly disappeared and I resented my time at Aunt Mabel's because I was forced to attend a church style and community I was unfamiliar with.

Having to pick between my foster mother, church, and biological family was no easy task and a position I wouldn't want for anyone.

Seven-Day Notice

Summer was my favorite season of the year until I moved into Aunt Mabel's. The time living with my foster mother felt like an ice-cold summer. Although I only lived with her for two years, it felt like two lifetimes. Aunt Mabel had a persuasive way of hurting Mallory and me that started with her telling me, after looking through our files, that my sister Ebony did not share the same father.

This was followed by her constant manipulation due to the animosity between her and my mother.

The icing on the cake was my eighth-grade graduation. I was ecstatic to be graduating middle school and transitioning into high school even though things were not perfect. Aunt Mabel made a big scene because she felt I did not introduce her to my mother.

"All the things I've done for you, and this is the thanks I get?" She rambled on as I sat quietly trying to think about what I did wrong. The next morning, she contacted DFS and gave me a seven-day notice.

A seven-day notice is a request to put the child you're fostering into another foster care family. I went into high school with the immense trauma of moving into another family, but thankfully my next home was much better. There, I regained my love for warm summers. Things seemed on the upside, and the sun refreshed and warmed my soul.

PART THREE:

2005−2009

CHAPTER 9

TAG, YOU'RE IT!

The Great Wall of Fury

"*Hey!* What are you doing?"

The hallway door slammed open, stopping me in my tracks. Mr. Downing's presence and fast pace startled me. He seemed as though he had been on his way somewhere.

My eyes widened as I looked up at him. His grey button-up suit stared me dead in my face. He was one of the new computer teachers; I learned later that his name was Mr. Downing. My life flashed in front of me, heart beating faster as the big black Sharpie hit the floor, quickly retracting from my fingers. Forgetting to come up with a Plan B in case someone interrupted Plan A, I looked up and stared trouble right in the face. I had just been caught writing "A-dogg was here" in big black letters across the wall to symbolize my frustration for the abrupt changes that occurred at my school, such as the building being split into separate, smaller schools.

That fall day was a brisk one. I had just started my senior year of high school, which was more bitter than sweet. During my junior year, I learned that West Roxbury High would be broken up into four smaller schools; therefore students needed to prepare for a quick transition in time for senior year.

The teachers and administrators insisted this would be the right move for our well-being, but at the time I did not know exactly what that meant. I was more concerned about how this change would impact my relationship with my friends and teachers, and having to start something new. I would no longer be graduating with the class I entered high school with, and the lack of transparency around the entire process added extra anxiety, as it was yet another disruption in my life.

Along with these abrupt changes, I entered my last year of school not on track to graduate. While most students were focused on college prep and thinking about their next steps, I was not on track to do any of those things. I still hadn't passed the standardized Massachusetts Comprehensive Assessment System (MCAS)—a standardized test required for graduation. I only had one more shot to pass the test if I wanted to graduate, and getting caught writing on the wall did not move me any closer to this goal, or so I thought.

Thinking quickly on my feet, I yelled out, "I'm so sorry, I'm so sorry!"

I hoped I could get out of this one. "I promise I am going to clean it up!"

"No wait, come back!" he shouted as I ran off in the opposite direction, heading to the bathroom to grab some paper towels and water to clean it up.

Quickly escaping his wrath, I ran down the stairs from the fourth floor in a panic, out of breath. I soon realized that cleaning up permanent marker with water and brown paper towels would not do the job, but it was too late to return so I roamed my stomping grounds instead. There were no classes nearby or teachers to take notice that I was out of class without a hall pass, making it safe.

Walking alongside the railings, I heard a softer voice below. I was on the second floor overlooking the main floor when I saw this curly-headed, white-haired lady looking up at me from below.

"Excuse me?" said Dr. Ferrer, my new high school principal.

"Yes?" I asked, feeling a bit of hesitation.

"Have you seen a student by the name of Amnoni Myers?"

"*Nope!*" I said confidently and dashed away in the opposite direction. The principal probably didn't know if I was a student at her school or assumed I had a hall pass. To my advantage, the principal was new, and she didn't really know any of the students (yet).

Feeling like I was in hide and seek mode, I quickly made my way to the other end of the hallway on the main floor to avoid running back into Dr. Ferrer. Walking toward the auditorium, I peeked inside and saw students gathered there for class. I strolled in, moving toward some people I knew, and hid under the chairs, hoping not to get caught.

Moments later, I was greeted by one of the school police officers. He gazed over me as if he'd just caught a fish— mission accomplished. Getting caught by the school police meant I was in big trouble. I was not prepared. I had just told the principal that I did not know a student by the name of Amnoni Myers, and yet here I was about to meet her for the first time. I was riddled with nerves. Ironically, I was standing next to where, on a different floor, I was accused of assaulting a white teacher during my junior year.

I had been bullied by a student I thought was my friend but who turned out to have ill intentions toward me. She followed me through the hallway one afternoon, repeatedly screaming how I was a "bastard baby" and how my mother didn't love me because I was in foster care. I tried so hard to ignore her since I sure as hell didn't have a comeback, but I could feel the rage heighten each time I heard, "That's why your mother doesn't love you."

A teacher walked by and quickly interjected by standing in between us. I began to get louder now that he was there. Out of nowhere, a yellow pencil flew through the air and hit me in the head.

"*Move!*" I screamed at the teacher, barging through his hands as he tried to hold me back against the other student. He prevented her from catching these hands. Not realizing my strength at the moment, I pushed into him too hard, and he lost his balance and fell against the wall.

Anxiously awaiting my fate, I learned the next morning that I would probably be expelled and the teacher was looking to press charges against me. After speaking with an administrator about what happened, they urged me to write a letter to the teacher apologizing to him in hopes this would change his mind about pressing charges against me. I jumped on writing the letter to him, because that would mess up my opportunity to attend college and I truly could not afford to have a criminal record.

He accepted my apology, and as a result the administration placed me on schoolhouse suspension during the week. I was sent to the Barron center on the weekends, which was an alternative school for students who typically fight, bring weapons, and are considered the worst of the worst. I was not the most excited about going to school on the weekend, but because the administration made an exception for me to stay in school, I did what I could to turn the situation around.

I appreciate that things did not go far worse for me, but part of me has to acknowledge that not all students know how to advocate for themselves. A student should not be put in a position where their life can be turned upside down over a mistake.

Anxious and shaking after being found in the auditorium during my senior year, the school officer and I walked hand in hand to the principal's office. I was already on my last suspension, as I'd been suspended a few times before this. I hoped and prayed she would not call my foster mother, because I did not want to be reminded of what I'd done and I couldn't afford to end up on punishment again.

Knots bunched at my stomach and throat. I knew I was walking into a bad situation. I felt very anxious sitting before my principal and Mr. Downing. I was so irritated at him; why would he snitch on me like that? *He probably don't even like black people like the rest of them*, I thought, but I was overall annoyed that I couldn't easily get away with something for once. It felt like I could never catch a break.

A Second Chance

I sat, my head facing the floor, not wanting to meet their eyes. Part of me wanted to go off so they could just hand me my sentence. I couldn't bear the awkward silence. I just wanted them to get on with it.

And then I heard Mr. Downing ask: "So what do you like to do besides drawing graffiti on the walls?"

Dr. Ferrer chuckled with her arms crossed.

I chuckled back, shrugging my shoulders. "I don't know."

I don't remember all that I said, but for some reason their question calmed me. I remember briefly talking about being in foster care, how my college essay writing process was going, and what my plans were after high school. I did not have a clear vision of what to do with my future, but I felt determined to do something different.

Leaving that meeting, I felt different compared to the other times I had been in trouble. The adults in my life were not always interested in what I wanted or needed, but Mr. Downing and Dr. Ferrer seemed to care. The way they spoke showed me I mattered beyond the bad mistakes I had made. Although I annoyingly had to wash all the walls in the school for community service, I was happy I could dodge suspension. They also put a plan in place for Mr. Downing to work with me on writing my college essays and, as awkward as it was, we slowly developed a friendship.

I left the office feeling much better, knowing I had a plan in place to cross the finish line. The genuine care and concern Mr. Downing and Dr. Ferrer showed me at that moment went beyond their words. They sprang into action to make sure I was on track. I wasn't just some aimless person walking around with a chip on my shoulder to them. I mattered, and I was not used to that. Having often felt invisible, I left that meeting with the sense that they were going to have my back.

About a week later, I took Mr. Downing up on his offer to sit down with him on a weekly basis. Along with him, I'd recently met someone at my church who took me under their wing to help me prepare for life after graduation. This overwhelmed me, to say the least. For so long I had played it off like I didn't need the help, procrastinating, but deep down inside I struggled with how administrators and teachers treated me.

"I saw you as a student who had been left behind, going unnoticed," Dr. Ferrer later shared as I questioned her about why she took the time to get to know me and help me.

Although I grew up hearing positive and uplifting messages from the church, I often saw myself on the other side of those collective messages given how my life situation did not fit with the status quo. While I sought positive interactions with adults, it proved easier to gain their attention through my negative behavior. There were so many complex pieces to me, as I was battling low self-esteem and doubt. It was easier to hear myself counteract, «Amnoni, you can do this," with "Amnoni, *no you can't!*»

Honestly, it felt foreign and uncomfortable to hear, but gradually I accepted the positive messages for myself, slowly gaining more confidence. I'm glad I was able to receive the help I needed, but also that caring adults invested the time and energy to provide a safe environment for me to share my concerns and have a consistent adult figure I could rely on. Believing in a young person is something very easy that everyone can commit to. As a young person, this moment made me feel I mattered. It started with Mr. Downing and Dr. Ferrer treating me with respect and asking me a question about how I acted rather than assuming and automatically punishing me. Through this experience I turned to writing my feelings out in essays instead of writing on the walls.

CHAPTER 10:

THERE IS A GOD!

The time of the year came when most students start to get their acceptance or rejection letters from colleges and universities. A long piece of construction paper filled the white walls with huge letters written across it, "C-O-N-G-R-A-T-U-L-A-T-I-O-N-S class of 2006!" Here, students' achievements were recognized, showcasing what colleges and universities they were accepted to. I was desperate to see my name appear with a list of schools I'd been accepted to, but the empty spaces remained empty since I was still in the applying phase. Next to the congratulations banner was my guidance counselor's office, where I stopped by to inquire about an application fee waiver and assistance with applying to the local college, Salem State University.

"Hi! Ms. Maria," I said, walking into her office bubbly and excited, "can you help me apply to Salem State, please?"

I wasn't too keen about applying to the school, but this was one of the few options I felt I had besides the community colleges I applied to. Looking at me, Ms. Maria frowned and began spelling out in a soft voice the laundry list of reasons why I shouldn't apply.

"Your GPA is too low. You should start off at a community college," she said, along with a host of other things, insinuating that providing me with an application fee waiver would be a waste of time.

"I don't care; I still want an application," I said before storming out of her office to look for Dr. Ferrer.

"Dr. Ferrer, can I please talk to you?"

"Sure, sweetie, what's going on?"

"When I asked Ms. Maria if she could help me apply to Salem State, she told me I didn't qualify and refused to give me an application fee waiver."

Met with disbelief as her eyebrows raised, Dr. Ferrer grabbed my hand, walked down toward her office, and assured me that she would figure this out.

Walking back down the stairs to Ms. Maria's office, Dr. Ferrer confidently walked right through the doorway with me standing behind her, with her hands on her hips and a raised tone.

"Maria, did you tell Amnoni that she could not apply to certain schools?" she asked.

Puzzled and not knowing what to say, we just looked at each other for a silent moment. Dr. Ferrer continued, barely giving Ms. Maria the opportunity to explain herself.

"You are not allowed to tell a student where they can and cannot go!" The room felt tense as Dr. Ferrer turned to me, softly, "Hun, what colleges are you thinking of applying to?"

"Um, Salem State . . . ?" I responded hesitantly. I knew they required a 3.0 GPA and at this point I only had a 2.3 GPA.

Dr. Ferrer turned to look at me. "That's a great choice!" she said.

Dr. Ferrer stood up for me when I needed her most, and I was thankful. Although my determination to apply was amplified when Ms. Maria refused to help me, I was thankful to have a principal who put the needs of her students first. I was tired of fighting this battle alone. My journey to graduate from high school wasn't an easy one, but things started shifting drastically in my favor.

A New Trajectory

Over the next few months, I worked hard to prepare for the MCAS test since this was my last chance to take it. I couldn't understand why after three years of trying I was met with failure each time. How could I not pass the exam even when I cheated? Can you imagine cheating and still not passing? I had to prove—not only to myself, but to my foster mom, my church family, and others—that I could pass this thing.

I needed to submit my college applications, adding pressure to pass the test. Otherwise, they wouldn't consider me without that score. I couldn't rely on my SAT or ACT scores because they were so low. I also had a 2.3 GPA. Even though I raised my GPA during my final semester in high school, it didn't matter. Schools only looked at the grades from the first semester of your senior year and your junior year. I felt like I had so much to lose, but at the same time I was determined and adamant about passing. I had a graduation to get to.

Unlike previous years when students had to stay after school to attend the MCAS prep sessions, Dr. Ferrer set it up so students could prep two days a week. The vice principal, Mrs. Wilson, was charged with supporting the handful of students who still needed to pass. I was pulled out of French class on Tuesdays and Thursdays until the time came to take the exam. As the exam grew closer, she provided optional weekend sessions where she worked with us. It started off with other students showing up, and then it was just me.

In those moments when I showed up alone, Mrs. Wilson would say, "Your determination is what's going to help you pass this exam. You got this."

Easily becoming overwhelmed with some of the simple math, I would beat myself up and get upset. She'd get me a drink, like hot chocolate, and say, "Don't worry. Let's take a break."

The best part of going to her house was that she was a good cook. She would have food prepared. We would stop and eat, and then continue to work.

The day for the MCAS test finally arrived! I was so nervous when I woke up, the time it took for me to prepare just seemed to fly by. I really, really, really hoped I would pass this time. I prayed and asked for guidance. I knew if I didn't pass, I wouldn't be able to graduate. This day was my only chance. Stepping into the room, we got a pep talk reminding us to breathe through the exam. My legs shook as my pencil tapped the desk. I tried not to doodle. This time I kept my eyes on my own paper.

Slowly but surely, I worked through the questions. I took a few breaks here and there, and then got right back to work. The environment felt different this time; it felt supportive. Every so often Miss Wilson would look up at us and say, "You got this!" This ongoing encouragement helped me push forward.

Lo and behold, about a month later, the test scores arrived. I was actually standing in the same spot as I had been when Dr. Ferrer, Mrs. Wilson, and another SPED teacher had gathered around me as we tried to make a decision as to whether or not to apply for a waiver so I didn't have to take the MCAS.

Apparently, there was an extension in place for those who had a learning disability. If I had known about the extension three years ago, I would have gone for it. However, I didn't want the handout. I was too ashamed because getting the extension meant I didn't deserve to graduate, and I would have felt guilty about getting a pass. More importantly, I wanted to prove to myself that I could do it. I constantly got such modifications in the special education classes, which led me to feel as though the teachers only expected the bare minimum from me.

"Oh my gosh, oh my gosh, show me my test results!" I remember saying as I watched the excitement in their faces, as if they already knew the outcome.

"You passed!" Dr. Ferrer announced, handing me the results. "You not only passed, but you moved into the 'more than proficient' category!"

Shocked, I couldn't believe it. I studied the paper to make sure it was correct. It sure felt good to no longer see "needs improvement" on my test results.

"Can I call my foster mom?" I asked

"Of course, go right ahead," Dr. Ferrer replied.

I ran to Dr. Ferrer's office and picked up the phone to quickly dial her cell. The phone rang.

"Hello?"

"Hey, Michelle."

"Hey, Amnoni. How are you doing?"

"Guess what, I have some really good news for you."

"What is it?" she asked.

"*I passed the MCAS!*"

There was a silent pause over the phone.

"Oh my gosh, there is a God!" she shouted.

I laughed so hard when she said that because Michelle was not one bit religious. Hearing those words come out her mouth assured me that she was proud of me; Michelle did not always show her emotions.

I quickly appreciated and felt her gesture of excitement, but then I thought, *Wait a minute. You're that shocked?* I was surprised, but the depth of her shock felt condescending. The moment was bittersweet since I knew I had amazed a lot of people. At the end of the day, it felt good to say, "I told you so!" Deep down inside, I was tired of proving my worth to people.

This moment meant everything to me. I hit the mark and felt good about something I truly worked hard for in my educational career. It finally felt official to apply to colleges knowing I could send my MCAS test results. I was finally on track to graduate.

The consistent reassurance I received by this new administration felt quite different from previous years. Right before graduation, Dr. Ferrer put on an award ceremony for students. While I didn't receive any awards for merit, I received the "Most Improved Student" award, along with a special scholarship in honor of Dr. Ferrer's mother. I was one of few students to receive this recognition, and as I stood up to accept the award, I gave Dr. Ferrer a huge hug, walking back to my seat feeling like a prize.

CHAPTER 11:

THE ABRUPT TRANSITION

Like a slow leak, I dreaded the day I would turn eighteen.

I remember the feeling like it was yesterday. I received a call from my social worker informing me I was no longer going to be able to stay at my foster mother's home and I needed to come and get my stuff as soon as possible. I was in disbelief, confused, and life was yet again changing outside of my control.

How could this be happening? Just a few weeks ago I was celebrating my eighteenth birthday with a chocolate cake and eighteen birthday candles without knowing what my fate would be. I thought I was going to be signing back into foster care and residing with my foster mother, whom I had lived with for close to three years. I thought I was in a place where I could finally breathe—how could I be so stupid to not prepare? I should've been ready all along.

All throughout your childhood you look forward to your eighteenth birthday—your independence increases, and you can finally do whatever you want because you're an adult. But as a foster youth, turning eighteen meant that I aged out of the system. My bed at my foster mother's house was no longer paid for. I was on my own.

Each year about 23,000 foster youth "age out" of the system.1 This means they have no permanent legal connection to an adult, like an adoptive family, legal guardian, or their birth family.2 Many states have extended foster care so youth can remain in the system until they're at least twenty-one, maintaining access to services and support from the state.3

Unfortunately, that wasn't the case for me. I was on a path toward achievement, about to graduate high school and go off to college, but I still felt vulnerable and unprepared.

I wasn't just going off to college; I was going off to an intensive college prep program because my grades weren't good enough to go through the regular admittance process. In order for me to be accepted into the school, I had to have at least a 2.7 GPA. Coming out of high school, I only had a 2.3 GPA, so I was struggling to figure out how I was going to be able to survive this summer because the program was pretty rigorous and strict. We were in classes for most of the day. We were not allowed to leave campus, and we had a curfew. The program posed a learning curve, to say the least. I was not used to the new pace of learning.

Unlike high school, where the stakes felt lower, I now needed to read between sixty to eighty pages each night on top of completing other assignments. I wasn't used to handing in my assignments on time or sitting still in the classroom for long periods. There were so many expectations already built around me that the pressure in my pot was heavily simmering.

If I couldn't survive this program, I wasn't sure how I was going to be able to survive college. The stressors I experienced were a little more heightened because I was also carrying academic challenges. I knew I wasn't the greatest student, and my arrival to this program wasn't an easy one.

Then I received the call from my social worker that changed my life in a public way.

"Hey, Amnoni—it's Karen. I have some news to share with you really quickly."

I couldn't imagine what it could be.

"Unfortunately, Ms. Mitchell can no longer house you."

"What do you mean?" I asked. "She told me I could stay here through college."

"Unfortunately, this is no longer the case. She needs your bed."

I felt ashamed. I was lost. I couldn't stop thinking about what I had done to deserve this type of treatment as I stood in the lobby at the student center. Was I not a human? How was I supposed to get all my assignments done and find a ride to Boston to get my belongings? (This was before Uber and Lyft had arrived on the scene circa 2006.)

I was angry that I didn't have a say as to where I could go. The decision was made for me, as it had been when the Massachusetts Department of Children and Family Services took permanent custody of us. This was their MO, though. Complaints about the way they conducted business and their sorry excuses were often met with, "We are doing what's in your best interest."

The abrupt transition from childhood to adulthood was scary. No one told me what to expect. I was angry at the system, feeling as though they had dumped me. I was angry with my foster mother.

Suddenly, I didn't matter anymore. It seemed like she just needed to make room for someone else. It felt as though she was just doing it to collect a check. I had nowhere to turn, no close family members I could confide in. While my siblings were still in foster care navigating their own placements, our lives were less enmeshed once we separated so I felt more alone. While I should have been celebrating the fact that I was going off to college, I was met again with another roadblock.

Later that week I received special permission to return to the house to pack my belongings, but when I got to the door and saw my belongings all packed in two pink suitcases and black trash bags with red handle ties, I couldn't explain the magnitude of the frustration I felt, as if a ticking time bomb was about to explode inside of me.

As I've had more time to reflect, I realize I was frustrated that I never had the option to pack my own things. The way my things were just thrown into trash bags felt dehumanizing, as though the system had just thrown me away. My social worker didn't even come up to visit me to break the news. This experience contributed, and still contributes, to my low self-worth and how I feel about myself.

Celebrating developmental milestones was often blurred with reminders of not having my biological family by my side. I wanted to have those normal moments that other kids had, surrounded by so many other people in their families, but my mother and father didn't show up for me on my first days of anything.

When I moved into college, they didn't help me go school shopping for my things. They didn't help move me in.

I developed a disdain for the system. It took me away from my family and never returned me. It left me to fend for myself. Despite the betrayal I felt, there was nothing left to do but keep going and find my way. Temporarily staying with my aunt that summer, I forged a path to keep going because getting a final acceptance letter into one of the few schools that initially accepted me felt like my only hope.

It just so happened that all of my hard work paid off. I surpassed the GPA requirement and was officially accepted into Salem State College.

In the United States, the age of majority is not the same as the age of self-sufficiency. Over half of youth ages eighteen to twenty-four report living with their parents.4 The federal government even allows youth to remain on their parent's health insurance until age twenty-six through the Affordable Care Act. For foster youth, by the time they reach twenty-six, only three to four percent will have earned a college degree.

Youth exiting the foster care system are expected to achieve independence at eighteen or twenty-one years old—that's five to eight years before their peers.

They often face challenges many adults will never encounter. According to a study by the Family and Youth Services Bureau, half of homeless youth interviewed reported being in foster care at some point in their lives. These youth tended to experience longer periods of homelessness than their peers who had not been in care.5 Twenty percent of nineteen-year-old current and former foster youth reported being homeless within the past two years. That number increased to twenty-seven percent for twenty-one-year-old survey participants.6

In contrast, youth allowed to stay in extended foster care with the proper supports, regardless of their race and ethnicity, often excel. They are more likely to graduate from high school and have full-time employment. They are less likely to be homeless and give birth and/or father a child at a young age.7 Research shows that current and former foster youth can thrive when given the opportunity and tools to do so.8 A history of overcoming adversity contributes to their resiliency. You should never allow your past to dictate your future.

CHAPTER 12:

TURNING POINT

Standing in front of the big glass window of my dorm room and looking outside toward the lake, I checked out my new surroundings, having just transferred from Salem State to Hampton University. Boats were coming in from every which way as if they were traveling toward the light. I couldn't quite enjoy the experience; I was overwhelmed with moving to an entirely new state and attending a new school. I could feel my chest getting tighter, my breathing getting heavier and my emotions swerving all around my head.

I think I'm having a heart attack, I thought. I considered calling Mrs. Karen, the new student administrator, for support. Thankfully, one of my friends lived down the hall and brought me to the medical center where I was met by the nursing staff.

"What's going on?" they asked as tears streamed down my face while I breathed heavily.

"I feel like I'm having a heart attack!" I said, clutching onto my chest.

"Okay, calm down," a nurse replied, bringing me into one of the rooms where she checked all of my vitals.

"We think that you should go to the hospital to do a further assessment. We don't have all of the tools to check certain things. We are going to call the ambulance for you."

"No! No, no, no! I think I'm okay. I really don't want you to call the ambulance because in my community we don't do that; it's too expensive," I replied.

Being out of state as a foster youth with Medicaid at the time was a death sentence because your health insurance wasn't covered if you went to school out of state. The nurses reassured me that I was going to be okay, so I agreed. Anxiously waiting for the ambulance to come, I could not help but think about all of the assignments I had to do since finals were approaching, but I was also fixated on the fact that any moment my chest could burst open. Shortly the ambulance arrived, and I was hauled into the back, alone and wishing that I wasn't alone.

"Please, please, please, *please* don't place the needle in my wrist," I said, as they tried to place an IV.

"We can't find one in your arm," they said as the paramedics tried to negotiate other areas of my body to accept the needle. They slowly moved closer to the top of my hand as I cried out even harder, clinging onto their arms.

"It's going to be okay, it's going to be okay," the two white men said, staring into my eyes.

Being carried out of the ambulance came with its own sort of judgment, as I did not want to be seen by others. Rushed to the back entrance of the hospital, I was placed in a room by myself. At least a few hours wandered by before doctors could evaluate my heart. Using the EKG machine, I was really nervous about what they were going to find. I thought for sure that I had clogged arteries.

Staring at the machine as the doctor pointed out different areas of my heart, he said, "Your heart looks great, Miss Myers."

That felt like a fresh breath of air but left me wondering what exactly was going on. Soon after the doctor came inside. "It sounds to me like you had a panic attack."

"What is that?" I asked, as he described the symptoms associated with it.

"It feels like you have a ton of bricks on your chest and you can't breathe."

That made sense and took me back to a similar feeling I had when I was at Salem State, when I found out my stepfather suddenly passed away to cancer.

I came back to the dorm room, avoiding looking out the window and resting my head on my pillow until the next morning when the sun beamed on my face.

I wondered how I was going to survive the rest of the semester at Hampton and keep my emotions at bay as I prepared for finals. I slowly began to realize that it wasn't as easy to just let things go as I had thought. Things I thought I was letting go of and praying away were actually being suppressed. I just didn't have the words to describe them. Thankfully, I was nearing the end of the semester and summer was upon me; I could get the break I needed. Through it all, I was able to pass all my classes and finals and received a surprise in my mailbox a few months later. It said: "Congrats, we are excited to announce that you made the Presidential Dean's List!"

What? I couldn't believe it. This was the first time I made it on anyone's Dean's list. Just a year ago, I was at Salem State barely surviving. I got mostly Fs and one B, so this was definitely a cause for great celebration despite the internal turmoil I was facing.

Arriving back home in Boston that summer, I was advised by a former mentor to see a psychiatrist because of the anxiety attack I experienced at Hampton.

"But why?" I whined. "Only crazy people see psychiatrists, and I am not one of them. I am a child of God."

Hampton University's administration, along with the school psychologist, advised me to find a consistent therapist to meet with on a regular basis in order to return the following semester.

I obliged and made an appointment that week with a psychiatrist. Entering Tuft's Hospital was pretty intimidating. *Isn't the hospital for sick people?* I thought, feeling vulnerable and more than a little unsettled. I didn't understand why seeing a psychiatrist was so important at the time until meeting him.

"Good evening, my name is Dr. Joseph Jankowski," a tall statue said, looking down into my eyes.

He was definitely more than six feet tall. His demeanor felt more like Mr. Rogers, who was a gentle giant. His voice was calm as he directed my mentor and me into his office. Dr. Jankowski was the head of the children's psychiatry department, and even though I was twenty years old, he still took me on as his client. The preliminary interview felt more like a conversation as he asked me multiple questions related to my background. Going deeper into my history, questions began to surface around my childhood.

"Have you ever experienced physical abuse growing up?"

"Yes," I answered.

"Sexual?"

"Yes."

"Emotional?"

"Yes."

The conversation lasted more than three hours as we drove deeper into some of my experiences. I was on edge the entire time, waiting to see what he came up with.

"Here is my assessment: You have post-traumatic stress disorder, panic anxiety, and major depression. I am feeling a little hesitant to diagnose you with attention deficit hyperactivity disorder just yet, because sometimes similar symptoms can show up."

It felt like being hit with a ton of bricks. I was shocked, but it also felt like the first time I could breathe in a very long time. Finally, things were beginning to make sense. Even though I had been in counseling most of my life, I'd never been diagnosed with any mental health conditions.

I didn't have much awareness about what depression, anxiety, or PTSD truly looked like. I didn't know how they contributed to the imbalance of my emotions. Did this explain what happened when I couldn't breathe in my dorm room?

For a really long time, I just prayed things away. I believed that the things I went through were just things that were made to make me stronger. I had no idea that those things were actually eating into what I was trying to become. For many people who receive a diagnosis like that, there's a lot of shame and embarrassment associated with it even though one in five adults in the US experience a mental illness each year (Mental Health America, 2020) (National Alliance on Mental Illness, 2020).

This experience was the first time in my life when I realized that I needed extra support to really help me manage the trauma I experienced, because I went through life just surviving. I went through life trudging through the really difficult experiences, thinking I just didn't have enough faith.

What these diagnoses did for me was help create a new language and a better understanding of how I could begin to heal.

Dr. Jankowski placed me on a low-dosage medication that supported all three diagnoses. I started to see him every week, and after a while of that I transitioned to meeting with him every month. Little by little, I started to see some improvements. I was calmer, I could get out of bed most mornings, and I felt better about the direction I was heading in. If there were times when I needed emergency appointments, he was there. He sat and listened to me, and he helped me make meaning out of my suffering. By putting words to experiences I was not sure how to articulate, he validated that I wasn't alone.

What I found to be super important was that he also reminded me of my strength, drive, and determination to receive help, which so many people don't seek. He would say things like, "Amnoni, your story amazes me; you have just been through so much and haven't given up."

Part of my resilience was attributed to relying heavily on my faith at the time because that was what was expected of me. Most importantly, Dr. Jankowski met me where I was, and this was not something I was used to. He knew that I wanted to finish college so he saw the trajectory of where I wanted to go and made every attempt to work with me to get there.

Around this same time, the family I was living with told me about a free Christian counseling program for young girls and women who were at a crossroads in their lives. It was a six-month intensive treatment program and they wondered if I was interested in applying. I immediately said yes. I was so desperate for help and for my circumstances to change that I was willing to do anything.

The application process was in-depth, starting with filling out an application, completing weekly assignments, and doing several interviews. The program was highly competitive, and often there was a waiting list. Part of the decision-making process depended on how fast you could complete all the steps. Some girls were on the waiting list for months at a time. I was determined to not be on the list that long, so I completed each step pretty quickly. Even the staff was surprised. I applied in August, got accepted in September, and received my placement in October. I arrived in Monroe, Louisiana on October 31, 2008.

Even though I was not the most excited about having to take a semester off from school, I looked at this as an opportunity to help move me forward in life. Being in a community that mirrored some of my own experiences helped make the process a bit easier. Though it was not an easy journey, especially being one of two Black girls in a predominately white home, I had to adjust to things I was not used to—one being my hair. I'd recently started my hair locking journey and was in a place where it was especially difficult to get my hair done. Often, volunteers came in and offered their services but they didn't know how to do Black hair.

"Why don't you just cut off your hair?" I remember one of the staff members asking me. In disbelief, I was angry that those words were uttered from her mouth.

"Because it's my hair," I said back in an annoyed tone.

I was happy to have Stephanie, the other Black girl in the program, because anytime I needed my hair done, she would help me retwist it. Of course, we had to ask permission, since one of the program rules was that we were not allowed to touch each other.

Through it all, the program was the right journey for me at that time. I slowly began to appreciate being able to take a break and really focus on myself. While I initially came to deal with the depression and anxiety, I realized that I was dealing with deeper issues such as my history of sexual abuse, the rejection and abandonment from my parents, and the trauma I faced when I aged out of the foster care system and beyond. Here, I read books such as *Beauty for Ashes* by Joyce Meyer, who shared in her own personal journey of sexual abuse that some of the feelings I'd experienced around it were not as lonely as I thought.

The way I expressed love was doing things so that people could love me. I didn't realize I was worthy of love just because of who I am as an individual; I was so often made to feel my existence was a burden. This was the first time I realized as long as I was open to receiving support and help, I could bring those tools back into my daily life so I did not have to end up back in this place again.

Although this journey was a difficult one, it was one where I began to find out more about myself. I was able to find out more about others. And most importantly, that I was capable of moving through really difficult experiences and feelings.

There was a time when I struggled to understand the meaning of joy. In class, teachers talked about the difference between happiness and joy. I honestly didn't know the difference. Happiness was described by temporary things while joy was something more internal and lasting. I desperately wanted to know and feel what joy was all about, so I continued to pray and pray.

I began to read affirmations over myself from the book *God's Creative Power Will Work for You*:

"No weapon formed against me shall prosper, for my righteousness is of the Lord. But whatever I do will prosper for I'm like a tree that's planted by the rivers of water (Isaiah 54:17; Psalms 1:3)."

"I am delivered from the evils of this present world for it is the will of God (Galatians 1:4)."

"I am an overcomer and I overcome by the blood of the Lamb and the word of my testimony (Revelation 12:11)."

"I will do all things through Christ who strengtheneth me (Philippians 4:13)."

Typically, I struggled to get out of bed in the morning. I procrastinated on getting up since I was not looking forward to another day. Sleeping on the bottom bunk, I'd look up at the slats of the top bunk thinking about how I was going to tackle the day.

The morning after I read my first affirmation was very different from my typical morning. I woke up and remembered feeling this sense of joy that I hadn't really felt before. There was a different kind of feeling when I could roll right out of bed feeling really good about the day. I began to feel the words I was speaking and myself growing with confidence.

I had to stay an extra month because the program did not think I was quite ready to graduate with my peers, so I spent the extra month continuing the treatment program. I was initially upset that I could not graduate with the people I came in with, but I also knew I wasn't quite ready to go out and navigate the world. Seven months later, I was ready to graduate. I was excited to see the changes that I had made and ready to see those things reflected outside of the program. I graduated with my head held high, feeling more motivated and inspired to move on to the next phase of my life.

PART FOUR:

2014–PRESENT: SUNFLOWERS SPRANG UP IN IMPOSSIBLE PLACES

CHAPTER 13:

YOU ARE THE EXPERT

Monumental Figure

I met Ivette at a Christian conference during one of the lowest points of my life. She was a recruiter for the Christian Leadership Institute program looking for talented individuals who were interested in learning about leadership in Colorado Springs.

I connected with Ivette in the beginning of the New Year, and it was a vulnerable time for me. I'd recently been kicked out of a family that I had been connected with for over five years, and the anxieties around how I would define the meaning of home did not feel clear. As a young person who survived the foster care system, I learned very early I needed to be one step ahead of the game.

While holidays present so much hope for others, this holiday season was an overwhelming time for me as I was heavily focused on how to navigate finding stable placement during the holiday and summer breaks.

Ivette and I were among the few people of color at this predominantly white event. Her spirit was gentle, which made it easier for me to open up, and I felt a connection between us. I didn't always know how to answer questions when it came to describing the complexities of my background to people. However, it was easy for me to share with Ivette that I'd grown up in foster care.

At the time, I didn't realize this interaction would change the trajectory of my life. This was when Ivette shared with me that she had just met Rebecca, a young woman who was a former leadership student but now worked as a policy director for the Congressional Coalition on Adoption Institute (CCAI). During the conversation, Rebecca shared with Ivette about her work with the Foster Youth Internship Program in DC and Ivette thought I would be the perfect fit. I remember her saying, "It's really prestigious," and "Congress needs to hear your voice."

Inspired and intimidated, I couldn't really think that far in advance but I was open to anything different from where I was. I didn't think I would get accepted into the program, but the summer after I graduated from college, I found myself interning on Capitol Hill in Washington, DC.

"You are the expert, an advocate. We are relying on you to tell us what changes the system needs," was the sentiment the CCAI staff shared with us, the lucky twelve who had been accepted into the Foster Youth Internship Program, often referred to as FYI. I was puzzled by this statement. This was one of the first times I had seen myself as an expert and advocate. This moment brought me back to when I was a child sitting in the chair as Granma combed my dark, black, beautiful hair telling me, "Your life experiences will matter one day."

As a child, I couldn't quite comprehend the meaning of her words, but as I stood on Capitol Hill I began to understand the possible power of my voice. I grew up in a community where everyone had it rough, so what made me so special? I often felt guilty about being one of the ones who "made it out," but I continued to remember that I had finally been given a chance to bring my voice to something I deeply cared about.

As there was much excitement around this new opportunity, I was also overcome with feelings of inadequacy, disbelief, and constant wondering about whether I was an actual imposter. How did I go from being a kid who grew up in foster care, becoming homeless while I was in college, to standing in the midst of powerful people? My world suddenly turned into a life I never imagined having.

As part of the internship I was placed in the office of Senator Chuck Grassley, a Republican from Iowa. I spent the summer working with his team on key issues related to foster youth. This gave me the opportunity to provide fresh insight about the experiences that many young people in foster care face.

Working in a Republican office was an adjustment. I often felt resentful that I wasn't placed as one of the Black caucus members. However, what kept me grounded was that Senator Grassley was co-chair and founder of the Senate Caucus on Foster Youth, a powerful bipartisan group dedicated to improving the child welfare system.

During the course of my internship, I began to share parts of my experience with Senator Grassley's senior legislative assistant. She spoke with Senator Grassley, who then asked if he could highlight my story on the Senate floor. While I was nervous about sharing my story so publicly, I was filled with excitement that my aging-out experience would be shared publicly in hopes of helping others.

Even though it was my story to tell, I was worried about how my mother would react if she heard on C-SPAN about how I was abandoned by her at the hospital. I called my mom to share the news and check in to see how she felt. She reassured me that by telling my story I was going to help others not make the same mistakes she did. She told me that I should share it. While it felt good to hear her say that, I wondered how she felt deep inside.

On the evening before Senator Grassley was set to give his speech, I randomly sent a text message to Ivette telling her that Senator Grassley was going to be sharing my story on the Senate floor. I thought she was home in Colorado, but she quickly replied that she was in Washington, DC. I was shocked—it was such a perfect coincidence!

Taking a deep breath, Ivette and I stood side by side taking photos and reflecting back to the day she met me two years prior.

"Amnoni, remember when you describe your life experiences as monumental? Well, the day has arrived my darling!"

I never thought a day like this would come, and even through the many conflicts I felt about this day I was determined to use this platform to bring about sustainable change. As Ivette sat in the House Chamber watching from above, Senator Grassley and I approached the Senate floor and walked toward the microphone.

Feeling like a mini-celebrity as all eyes landed on me, I was overcome with chills and a stomach full of emotions. I stood in a place I never thought I would see. Typically, the Senate floor is reserved for powerful people while others only get the chance to view the experience through television.

The smell of the wooden furniture permeating the room reminded me of the church pews back home. My eyes widened, taking in the moment as if it were my last. I looked around like a kid in a candy store.

On July 7, 2014, Senator Grassley shared my story with the members of the United States Senate:

Mr. President, for many years, I have been an advocate for reforming the foster care system and making sure the government is doing the best it can to protect and care for those who are abused, neglected, and removed from their families. That is why Senator Landrieu and I started the Senate Caucus on Foster Youth. We wanted a forum to discuss policies and practices and to learn more about the challenges that foster youth face. We want to make a difference in the lives of vulnerable youth who don't have a permanent place to call home. The Caucus cannot function without the input and insight from foster youth. These children are the experts on the foster care system. They tell us what works or what needs to change. They share their experiences and provide us with real world stories about how our policies truly affect them.

Today, I want to highlight the story of one particular person whom I have had the privilege of getting to know. Amnoni Myers is an intern in my office this summer. She's participating in the Congressional Coalition on Adoption Institute's Foster Youth Intern program. I wanted to tell her story because it's important not to forget that there are children in this country, like Amnoni, who don't have a permanent family or place to call home. Despite her circumstances, Amnoni has risen up and made a better life for herself. So, allow me to share her story.

Even though she had a better family environment after placement, life still presented her with many challenges. Amnoni struggled with rejection and trauma at a very young age resulting from different types of abuse. One of the most difficult experiences Amnoni faced was aging out of the foster care system.

During the summer, while still in care, Amnoni entered into an intense college preparation program that would determine if she was adequately prepared to enroll in a post-secondary institution. Already anxious about the future of her success and if she would be able to handle the workload of the program, she received a phone call from her social worker that afternoon. She was told her foster mother was no longer being paid for Amnoni's bed. Because the money was running out for her foster mother, Amnoni was forced to leave the home immediately.

The shock and devastation of those words crushed Amnoni. She lived in that home with that family for three years. She considered it to be a long-term living situation. Amnoni returned to find her belongings packed in garbage bags waiting for her at the door. Amnoni aged out of the system in a way no person should ever have to experience. She left a place she considered home, not knowing what her future would hold. She was on her own, shoved into independence with no family, support, or a place to call home.

Amnoni's aging-out experience left her feeling shattered and confused. She felt betrayed by both her foster mother who claimed to love her and the child welfare system that claimed to protect her. While this experience quickly taught Amnoni the value of independence, she would have preferred to have a smoother transition into adulthood.

When Amnoni left her so-called home at age eighteen, she was taken in by her former mentor and her family. She resided there for five years. Living there was a reminder that love, family, and support do exist. Today, she is working in my office, sitting in this chamber, learning how the government works. She is becoming an advocate for foster youth who face the same experiences as she does.

Despite the challenges, Amnoni feels very fortunate. She has been able to attend college, graduate this year, and hopes to pursue a meaningful career. Knowing that many children and youth don't have adequate support systems in their life to help them along their life journey, Amnoni pursued an education in social work and sociology. Many people who have gone through similar experiences resort to other paths because of the lack of support and services they receive. Many foster children age out of the system without supportive services in place to ensure healthier lives. Thankfully, Amnoni has had a network of support to guide and direct her through these difficult times.

Amnoni's experience has fueled her passion to advocate for those who don't have a voice to fight for themselves. As Amnoni looks back on her life, she realizes her past does not have to determine her future. She is on her way to becoming a monumental figure for those who have suffered, giving youth across the country a voice and making a difference in this world. I appreciate Amnoni's willingness to let me share her story. She's a very brave woman. She knows we can learn from her. We must do right by her and others in the foster care system. I hope my colleagues have the chance to say hello to Amnoni while she's here, and take a minute to commend her for being an advocate for other youth.

The Senate chamber erupted in applause as Senator Grassley concluded his remarks and turned to look at me. Together, we walked off the Senate floor. My heart was full. I couldn't stop smiling in disbelief. Was this real life?

Life has a way of throwing you unexpected curveballs, and in the moment when you feel like your life is falling apart, sometimes a glimmer of hope comes knocking at your door.

Reflecting back to Grassley's statement, I can see the strength, determination, and resilience that dwelled within me. I was overcome with an enormous amount of gratitude to see and experience how the challenges I faced in care were being used to raise awareness and create change that could positively impact the foster youth coming behind me. The seeds of my past were beginning to flourish, and things in my life started to fall into place.

CHAPTER 14:

THE PEAK

Every year the Congressional Coalition on Adoption Institute (CCAI) holds a congressional briefing to give young people in foster care a chance to address areas where policies can be improved for the child welfare system.

During this time, trauma-informed care was a relatively new concept that slowly manifested in the child welfare community. I learned about trauma-informed care while completing my social work practice at GLIDE Memorial. The case manager team asked if I could present the organization with recommendations to provide compassionate care for clients who experienced trauma. I wanted to learn more about what trauma-informed care was and how the practices could translate to the child welfare system, so I wrote my policy report on the importance of training foster parents and caregivers about trauma-informed care techniques so that they were not causing more harm to their foster children.

What people don't always understand is that even if a child is living in an abusive environment, being removed from their biological family is still traumatic for them.

While I had mixed emotions about being separated from my mom, the grief and loss were compounded when I learned that my siblings and I were going to be separated. At the time, I didn't have the vocabulary to describe my emotions, and I struggled to reconcile why I was being taken out of one abusive environment only to be further abused when I went into foster care.

When I first began doing research, I only knew my own experiences and was not aware of the depth and complexities of all of the harsh realities young people faced in foster care. I didn't even know how many kids were in the US foster care system. The experience felt so isolating as a child, and I thought my siblings and I were the only ones. I learned that there were more than four hundred thousand kids in the system at any given time (Children's Bureau, 2018).

Growing up with these struggles, I also navigated between multiple experiences and identities I was not always aware of. I was not just a child. I was a Black foster child dealing with a number of traumas and developmental delays that stood in the way of me understanding the full extent of my trauma. But I was determined to write a different story for others, one that brought together innovation, sustainability, and something that would honor Ebony, who still struggled to find her way.

A Stone of Hope

Less than a week before we were scheduled to present our policy recommendations at a briefing for members of Congress, Becky Weichhand, the Interim Executive Director of CCAI, shared some unexpected news with the interns. I was on the edge of my seat, figuring out how to brace myself.

"So, we have a surprise for you all," Becky said slyly.

The CCAI staff had been bragging about our FYI class being one of the best classes, so I hoped it was something good.

"Because you all worked so hard this year, the White House reached out to us," Becky said. "They want you to present your policy reports to the Domestic Policy Council." A rush of excitement flooded the room as we all collectively shouted and screamed. My eyes lit up as the dimples on my face grew wider and I grinned from ear to ear. *I can't believe I'm about to present my policy report to the White House!* I thought. *Are we gonna get to meet Obama? Michelle?*

I couldn't quite contain my excitement and called Mr. Downing first to share the news! My hard work was finally paying off. All of those late nights Jane, Darrah, Kaylia and I spent working at the Foggy Bottom Whole Foods and the Starbucks at the George Washington Hospital, all those tears I shed because I did not feel capable of writing a policy report despite the encouragement I received—hearing that we were going to present our recommendations to two of the most powerful groups of people in the country (the US Congress and the White House) not only made it all feel worth it, but felt like icing on the cake. In moments like these, it was easier to accept my past and not be angry because I was finally seeing the light at the end of the tunnel.

One of my DC bucket list items was to see the newly placed Martin Luther King Jr. monument on the National Mall. An important and instrumental monument, Black people had waited a long time to see it and to see Dr. King honored. The best time to see all of the monuments on the National Mall was at night because the contrast between the dark sky and the lights illuminating the monuments brought each intricate detail to life. The phrase, "Out of the mountain of despair, a stone of hope" was carved into Dr. King's monument.

I couldn't stop staring at it. I had never heard this beautiful quote, but the meaning stuck with me. This statement summed up my past perfectly. I carried those words with me as an affirmation to give me courage for getting through my upcoming speech.

Running toward the Mountain Top

On the morning of the White House briefing, I woke up early, got dressed, and prayed that President Obama would be there to see me present. I took my time to ensure my scalp was greased, my ankles weren't ashy, and my clothes were ironed. I was excited to wear my favorite black, ruffled button-down shirt, black skirt, a pair of stockings, and black shoes. Mine was as fancy as a conservative outfit could be.

All of the interns met outside and split up, each riding in different Ubers. Our drivers dropped us off on Pennsylvania Avenue a few blocks from the White House. Standing in the line of the Eisenhower building, I eagerly waited for the line to move. Finally getting through the security clearance, I received my visitor's badge. I slipped it over my head as if I was the boss. I was overwhelmed to be in such a powerful place, showcasing my masterpiece.

"This meeting has the ability to change each of your lives," Becky shared as we waited for a staffer to escort us to the conference room inside the Eisenhower building.

The moment I had been waiting for was finally here. I was determined to speak from a place of power by sharing my personal story, which had not only impacted my life but so many others.

They guided us down a hallway and into a conference room. I looked around at all of the fancy and intricate surroundings, silently squealing with bliss. A long table stretched along the middle of the room. We each sat in a chair, making sure to stay in the order in which we would share our policy recommendations. The White House staff sat across from us and in chairs placed around the room. I was the second intern to share, counting down each second until it was my turn. They gave us two to three minutes to speak, but I took a little longer as Saint Jane, another intern, gave me her extra thirty seconds.

I began my speech.

Will today be the day? This was the question I often asked myself as I sat in the cold and dark basement as a little girl trapped without food, water, or light for hours. Knocking loudly to escape, hoping someone would hear: Will I ever eat? Will I survive? Will I ever see the light? Forgotten. As I tried to escape this pain that my aching stomach felt, sleeping seemed to be the only way. This neglect and abuse I experienced by my caregiver led me to question whether I was human, and if so, why was I created? My story isn't so unique because thousands of children experience this type of maltreatment each day, but what is so unique about this story is that I survived.

President Obama, over seventy percent of children entering the foster care system experience at least two forms of complex trauma. Unfortunately, these traumas can often worsen when the child enters the home, because foster parents are not properly trained on how to deal with trauma. Sadly, I entered into a foster home already experiencing multiple traumas, but my foster mother ignored them and continued to do more harm. She noticed that I was malnourished when I entered the home, but continued to chain lock the fridge as if I was an animal. If foster parents continue to parent without being trauma-informed, the rates of additional trauma, mental health medication prescriptions, and government spending will continue to rise. Shockingly, a study conducted by the Centers for Disease Control and Prevention (CDC) shows that adverse childhood experiences could decrease a person's life expectancy by as many as twenty years.

Thankfully, studies show that if a positive, understanding family emotionally supports a foster child, the biological effects of trauma on the brain do not remain permanent. Right now, there are no federal standards requiring states to train foster parents on trauma-informed care elements after they become licensed. This cycle cannot continue. Children not only deserve the right to live, but deserve to have caregivers who can properly care for them. Congress should require that states receive federal caretaker funds to implement trauma-informed care elements that best serve their population.

Congress should also amend the Foster Care Independence Act of 1999 to include standardized, ongoing trauma-informed training for caregivers. (Congressional Coalition on Adoption Institute, 2014)

Everyone in the room cheered and clapped as if I just hit a mic drop. It felt good to hear how engaged they were as gasps filled the air and heads nodded while I spoke.

Looking around the room, I knew I was on the right track. I prayed I didn't trip over my words—I tended to do that when I was nervous. Although President Obama couldn't be there, the next best person was Roy Austin, Deputy Assistant to the President on Urban Affairs, Criminal Justice, and Opportunity. Nailing my speech and hearing the Domestic Policy Council staff's positive response made me feel like I was on top of the world.

Before we left, the staff took us on a brief tour. While we didn't get to present directly at the White House, we each received White House chocolates and the opportunity to walk down the long red carpet President Obama walked on right before he gave his speeches.

I had one speech down, and one to go.

Walking over to Capitol Hill, we were now going to give the same speech to Congress. While I was sad that, unlike some of my fellow interns, my family members couldn't attend, I also felt more at ease sharing experiences that many of them did not know about.

Never in a million years did I think that little ole me would highlight my challenging experiences in a way that was seen as an asset.

Growing up, some supportive adults often told me that my experiences were going to turn into a testimony, that I would someday feel as though I had arrived. I still spent so much time during college beating myself up and worrying about my future because I didn't graduate on time.

I graduated at twenty-six and wondered if I would always feel left behind. So much of my life was about playing catch up, and for the first time I could appreciate and believe that I was right where I needed to be, that I was worthy of receiving good things. I saw the mountain top and I was running toward it, awaiting what was next.

CHAPTER 15:

THE WHITE HOUSE

Have you ever seen clips on *Buzzfeed* of former First Lady Michelle Obama answering questions from a group of cute little children in the audience of the White House?

Apparently, this event happens every year when White House staff members get to bring their children to work for the day. I'd always wondered how it was that children were able to get that close to her and ask whatever questions were on their minds, unfiltered.

Watching this experience on Buzzfeed through my computer screen was as far as I thought I would ever reach (feeling a little jealous, I might add, that I wasn't face-to-face with Michelle Obama). But little did I know that I would be staring right into the very eyes of those same children as I stood in the East Room of the White House podium, introducing First Lady Michelle Obama for the annual Take Our Daughters and Sons to Work Day.

When I first arrived in DC I was pulled aside by Irene, a beloved White House staffer who took me under her wing, and asked if I wanted to work on this initiative.

Having my voice at the table was important because I could speak to some of the hopes and wishes young people had, and I felt passionate about it. What made the event special this year was that the White House recognized and involved young people in foster care for the first time. Unlike other children who can go to work and shadow their parents, children in foster care do not usually get to participate, through no fault of their own.

This was something I understood all too well.

My various foster mothers rarely showed up for parent-teacher conferences, and I would never be allowed to visit their place of work. Seeing other children participate in special days with their parents made me feel unimportant and unworthy. I was just another shadow in the background.

Collaborating with Children Family Services of Washington, DC, and the Boys & Girls Clubs of America, I identified young people in the foster care system and paired them up with staff members. The team and I were intentional about making sure foster youth were prioritized when it came to matching them with members of President Obama's cabinet.

The Friday before the event I was out on Pennsylvania Avenue, taking a typical coffee break at Starbucks with a few of my "sista interns" after a long day at the office. We had just finished an intern series with Denis McDonough, President Obama's chief of staff, and I was fired up after his conversation about navigating leadership beyond the White House. Then I got a call from Irene asking about my whereabouts.

"Hey girl, where are you?" Irene said in a low tone quite different from her usual bright and cheery one.

"I went to grab a cup of coffee really quickly."

"Okay, hurry back," she said. The situation seemed urgent so I rushed back to the office as fast as I could.

I ran up the two flights of steps, trying to catch my breath. As I walked down the hallway Irene's head poked out the door as she waved her hand signaling for me to hurry. I was nervous; I wasn't sure if a task I completed wasn't done right, or if there was an important email I overlooked as I prepared for the big event next week.

She ushered me into Roy Austin's office—he was deputy assistant to the President. There were a bunch of staff who worked on the Take Our Daughters and Sons to Work Day initiative standing in a circle as if some sort of surprise was in wait. The conversation went something like this:

"Amnoni, the team and I have been really impressed with your work to help coordinate this day."

Where is this going? I thought.

"Each year, we select an intern to introduce the First Lady, and as a team we unanimously selected *you*. And we wanted to know if you would be interested in introducing her?"

Before I could take the next breath, the word *"Yes!"* burst out of my mouth. My face widened so much I could feel the stretch in my cheeks. My heart skipped several beats.

It felt incredible to be noticed and recognized by a staff member because I often felt like an imposter, out of place, feeling as though I didn't belong among the elite group of interns.

Although I was personally invited to apply to the White House internship program for my advocacy efforts on child welfare, I still felt like I didn't earn my place at the White House (even though I did).

Moments before going out on the big stage, I was waiting in the Green Room to meet First Lady Michelle Obama for the first time. Standing on the podium minutes before practicing my speech, I kept telling myself to slow down because I did not want to trip over my words during an open media press event.

I'd visited the Green Room plenty of times while touring, but had never occupied a space designated just for the First Lady and me.

At this time, I still wore dresses and makeup, and I was all dolled up wearing my Sunday best, feeling a little like royalty. Awaiting her arrival, I wondered what she looked like in person. Was her hair as beautiful as they say? Would she tower over me with her long legs and stature? How did she smell? Then her heels clicked away as she walked through the Red Room and Blue Room, getting closer and closer. I leaned over to see if I could get a glimpse of her face.

Before I could catch my breath, I saw a majestic being walk closer and closer to me as my eyes widened. *This is too good to be true*, I thought.

Speechless, all I could do was embrace her with a hug as I tried uttering words out of my mouth.

I tried to catch a whiff of her perfume since friends asked me to figure out how she smelled. I couldn't quite capture how she smelled, but her nails were on fleek—colorful, matching the color of her dress.

She quickly complimented me on my dress, saying, "We look like twins with our dresses," which added another layer to my confidence because I, being a tomboy, really was not interested by my dress but had compromised because of the occasion. We briefly spoke as I shared with her the advocacy work I was doing.

In my peripheral vision, a Nikon camera snapped photos as we spoke. *I hope he's getting all my good sides*, I thought. I could not take my eyes off of the First Lady.

Staring into the large crowd, lights, cameras, and the awestruck brown eyes of Black and brown children in the front row gleamed from the White House podium. This was a dream I could never have imagined.

Looking into the crowd, I locked eyes with the children, feeling as though I stared back at myself. I remember being right where they were years prior. The only difference was that while I had been sitting in the auditorium of my middle school, they were sitting in the East Room of the White House.

I experienced my own déjà vu.

At my own school, Paul Pierce, a former basketball player for the Boston Celtics, supported by his team members standing by, spoke from the stage about his early life growing up, his many successes, and life as a professional basketball player. I admittedly can't remember all that he spoke about. I just remember the impression he had on me as a young twelve-year-old who'd just entered the foster care system.

As a middle schooler, I remember feeling anxious, wondering if I'd ever make it or if I was going to make an impact on other young people. But I continued to look into Paul Pierce's eyes as he spoke, hoping that I would have my own momentous moment—and years later, I did.

As First Lady Michelle was answering questions from the youth, every few sentences or so she pointed at me and casually said, "Like Amnoni said," as if I was her example for doing the right thing.

Getting those shout-outs from her made me feel like I was an influencer in my own right. As the event came to a close, Michelle Obama walked toward me, embraced me with a hug, and told me she was proud of me. I didn't want to let her go and held her for as long as I could. The embrace was what I needed—and just like that, a group of children swarmed me as I reached out my arms openly welcoming each of them in.

I knew I made it when one of the children looked at me and asked, "Do you have the Secret Service following you?"

That was when I recognized the power my presence can have on a young person. I may not have always seen myself as the prize, but that day I did.

CHAPTER 16:

A WAKE-UP CALL

On November 15, 2017, my world came to a catastrophic halt. I received an unexpected call that forever changed my life—not the type of call you expect early in the morning or the type you'd wish on anyone or their family. Prior to the call I woke up abruptly, tossing and turning as if I was fighting through the difficult decision my partner at the time and I were about to make. Waking up, I walked to the bathroom, slowly remembering where my anxiety was coming from.

That evening, my then girlfriend and I returned from counseling, got into a heated argument, and talked about breaking up as we cried through the difficult decision. The week prior we were counting down the days until we sailed away to the Caribbean for vacation to commemorate my graduation from the National Urban Fellows program with my Masters. Unbeknownst to my girlfriend, I was planning on proposing to her. I had recently returned from my hometown, Boston, to purchase the ring I had picked out with Mallory's help, and the help of his two children and my mother. Ebony had also approved of the ring through text messages, equally sharing her excitement and pride.

"You know you're going to be my maid of honor, Sis," I typed.

She responded back in text with excitement, "Hell yeah, you know I got you, Sis!" I imagined her sappy Bostonian tone through the phone.

But a month later, when I returned to California, things changed. Before the night ended, I was met by devastation and heartbreak.

After using the bathroom, I walked back over to the bed, sat down, and contemplated whether or not I should text Ebony to explain what my partner and I were going through. Plus, we were long overdue for a sisterly chat, and it was time for Big Sis to check in. During these conversations we spent hours on the phone talking about everything under the sun, including my relationship.

Before I could make the call, flashing lights appeared on the ceiling, reflecting my phone where it lay on the wooden table in the distance. I don't remember the exact time, but it was too damn early for people to be calling my phone.

Oh, no. This can't be good. It must be Ebony or my mother, I thought as I saw my older sister's name flash across the screen with each ring. Calls from Tiffany were unusual, and this call came at 2 a.m. Pacific Time where I lived and 5 a.m. Eastern Time where my family lived. Something was just not right.

Nervous and anxious, I quickly picked up. "Hello," I said faintly, trying to shield my voice as my partner lay sound asleep a few feet away.

"Hey Sis, how are you doing?" Tiffany replied. I could hear a commotion in the background as she tried to attend to the needs of my nephews. I heard my youngest nephew in the background asking if "Aunty Moni" was on the phone.

"Hurry up and get dressed," she said with a loud, raised voice. She sounded distraught and riddled with impatience. She began asking me questions.

"Where are you?" she asked. "Where is your partner?"

"I am in my room and she's sleeping," I replied.

"Are you sitting down?" she asked.

"I don't need to sit down," I anxiously replied, fearing the worst. "Please, just tell me."

"Are you sure?"

"Yes!" I shouted.

"The sheriff's department stopped by Mom's house this morning. They found Ebony unconscious. She had bleeding on her brain and she also had a heart attack."

I crumbled in disbelief, screaming about her whereabouts. "Is she okay?"

"It's Auntie Ebony," Tiffany said to the kids who were likely circling around her, trying to process the information as well. "Amnoni, they've taken her to the hospital and they don't know if she is going to make it."

I was overcome with so many emotions. I told Tiffany that I had to call her back. By this time, my partner heard me and rushed to my side. She asked me about what was happening. I could barely explain. I just started screaming, "I need to call Mr. Downing, I need to call Mr. Downing!"

Somehow dialing his number, I screamed into the phone, mixing up words as I tried to figure out what to say.

"They found Ebony, they found Ebony," I repeated the story my sister had just shared. Profusely apologizing, he asked what could do to help.

"I don't know what to do," I told him. "I don't know if I should fly home or wait here until I get an update. I don't want to miss her if I fly there." I could barely get another word out as I trembled and grabbed my face. My partner sprang up from the bed and into action. She took the phone and spoke with Mr. Downing. Together they came up with a plan to get me home to Boston.

This can't be happening, I thought. I saw my world crash in front of me. Not only was I about to lose the love of my life, but I was also losing my little sister and best friend all in the matter of a few hours. All I wanted was for the director of this horror film to come and yell, "*Cut!* We finished the scene; let's get back to work."

None of that happened. My body, mind, and spirit wavered in shock as I tried to piece together what happened to Ebony. I tried to avoid the reality that my little sister was slipping into an everlasting eternity.

Approximately six hours and three thousand miles later, I landed at Boston Logan Airport, anxiously waiting to meet Mallory. I walked into Brigham and Women's Hospital holding out hope that Ebony was going to pull through. Ebony was a fighter and had faced near-death experiences before, so I was hopeful she wouldn't succumb.

On the way from the airport, Mallory shared that Ebony had experienced several heart attacks. They were stabilizing her, and she was making a little bit of progress. But the scene looked entirely different when I walked into the Intensive Care Unit.

My family was in the waiting room, and they watched me walk to the back where Ebony was. The nurse was talking to me, but I was preoccupied with the overwhelming thoughts of what I was about to see. There Ebony laid with her head turned toward the door, propped up by pillows because her head, neck, and upper body were very swollen.

"This is not my sister!" I shouted to the nurse, hesitantly walking toward her.

Ebony was lying there with tubes and patches, surrounded by ventilation machines and bandages. Her chest was moving rapidly, but I came to find out that the machines were breathing for her. I moved in closer, holding her hands as I examined her body. I looked for clues to understand what could have happened. Not wanting to let her go, I held her tighter. I begged her to wake up.

"Please, Sis, just wake up," I said. I pulled out my phone and scrolled to one of the last pictures Ebony and I took together. I showed the attending nurse, who was equally surprised.

"Wow, she is really beautiful, and looks very different from how she looks now," the nurse stated as she further apologized to us. I didn't want the nurse's lasting impression of Ebony to be one of her lying lifeless in this bed. Instead, I wanted her to know that Ebony was beautiful, petite, and nothing like this woman in the hospital.

Moments later, my father came into the room. This was the first time I had seen him in years. Just a few years prior, my father had slipped into a coma after experiencing a heart attack due to a drug overdose. Now he was accompanied by his best friend, who wheeled my father into the room to visit Ebony.

He quickly got up from the wheelchair and stood over the hospital bed, shaking his head as he uttered words to her. Soon after, he reached deep inside his pocket, pulled out a small, white napkin, and reached over her face to wipe the fluid-like tears from her eyes. I had never seen my dad show affection until now. He desperately hoped that Ebony felt us nearby.

I immediately became bothered and angry as I repeated to myself, "This is all Ebony ever wanted."

All she wanted was for my father to wipe away her tears and hold her. She desperately sought approval from others and longed to have my mother and father's approval. Now she was lying on death's door only to have our father show up a moment too late.

I paced back and forth, walking from the waiting room where my family had gathered. I wanted to spend as much time as possible with Ebony.

"Things are not looking good," the doctor said. "There's nothing more we can do." I stood by Ebony's side, holding her hand and waiting to feel her pulse. But the moment we dreaded was here.

We gathered by her bed, praying, crying, pleading, and hoping the doctors were wrong. There was still time for Ebony to wake up, and I prayed she would. I continued to look over at her vitals, confused about what all the numbers meant. The machine continued beeping rapidly like an alarm warning us that the end was near. Ebony's heart rate slowed down, and we braced for impact.

Beep . . . beep . . . beep. I listened to the sound of the machines surrounding her as I held her left hand. Our family huddled closer as streams of tears rolled down each of our faces. Faint cries and utters of "No, don't go" swept through the room. The end of Ebony's life became clear when an automatic voice coming from the room stated, so matter-of-factly: "Heart rate cannot be read; please disconnect the machines."

Ebony was twenty-seven years old when she suddenly passed away.

CHAPTER 17:

THE AFTERMATH

Ebony was my little sister, my first best friend, and the holder of all my secrets. When things were difficult, I knew I could turn to her. She often knew what to say even when I didn't always want to hear it. It felt like we were invincible when we were together because nothing could stop us.

From riding our bikes up and down the street together, to bickering, arguing, and quickly making up, Ebony had her way of doing things, and I had mine.

One of my fondest memories as a kid was Ebony and I playing house together. Ebony enjoyed making dolls out of paper while I preferred playing with the dolls that already existed. Strawberry Shortcake and my miniature Cabbage Patch doll, Chelsea, were my go-to choices, but Ebony was sure to teach me how to create them on paper even if I wasn't the best artist.

Often following her lead as she didn't let much stop her, Ebony was much more decisive than I was. As we grew closer, we also grew apart due to being physically separated and assigned to different foster care placements. I know I was shocked by being separated from Ebony, but I didn't fully realize the impact it had on us.

We had always bickered and argued like sisters do, but our separation from each other in foster care took things to another level. Outside of scheduled visitations, Ebony and I still met up to connect and see how the other was doing.

One summer, we rode the green line trolley and met at the Boston Science Museum, where the huge dinosaur statue resided. We didn't even make it inside the museum because our fight lasted longer than usual.

As I went to embrace Ebony, I saw that she had a huge bandage on her wrist. While asking her what happened she said that she fell. I asked to see her arm, skeptical about her initial story, and while showing it to me I saw a bunch of red cuts formed across her arm—as if she'd been cutting. My heart stopped at the thought—if she was cutting, she may face hospitalization for the first time.

I didn't know how difficult the separation would be for us until I became an adult. Sharing space and growing up together for ten years and then all of a sudden going from not sharing space with the person you love was more difficult than I imagined.

We remained close, but there were periods of strain due to our circumstances. What I will always remember about Ebony is that she loved deeply and was loyal to the people she cared about. She was someone you could count on in your time of need. Ebony was talented, unique, and lived life to the best of her ability. Her motto was, "Live life to the fullest, even when life feels difficult." Life was truly difficult for her. What amazed me about Ebony was that no matter what she experienced, she strove to live the best life she could.

I am careful to say that she lived to die. What I mean by that is she had hopes, dreams, and visions she anxiously anticipated, but the weight of substance abuse, domestic violence, mental health challenges, and complex trauma, to name a few things, led her down a path that quickly turned to quicksand. She fought so hard to escape a life not meant for her, not meant for anyone.

Ebony came into this world in pain and left the same way. She gained her angel wings at the age of twenty-seven on Wednesday, November 15, 2017.

My life has not been the same since.

The Postmortem Effect

At 3:26 a.m. I happened to check my email. My heart began to pound and my eyes widened as they scrolled across an email I'd been anticipating and dreading for months. Just a few weeks before, I had posted my frustration on Facebook about the long wait, writing, "Millions of babies have been born into this world within the last nine months, and the cause of Ebony's death is still unknown." And now there, in a sea of less important emails, was the subject line in black, bolded letters: *Ebony's autopsy results.*

My mother forwarded the email to me from the Massachusetts Medical Examiner's office, leaving the message field empty. Empty is how I felt when I opened up the results to a bunch of medical jargon, not really understanding what much of it meant; it felt like reading a foreign language. Quickly searching on Google for the medical terms, I soon found out that Ebony had overdosed. The truth of the matter is, I already knew the cause of Ebony's death. I just didn't know all the details surrounding it because all she left behind was a video clip in her phone, capturing some of her last words, which included, "I am tired."

While I always knew the day of her death would come, I never imagined it coming so soon. A few years prior, I sat in my therapist's office with tears in my eyes sharing that I wished Ebony would hurry up and die. I was frustrated that my relationship with her was slowly fading at the hands of her abuser; I couldn't live with the pain of her existence. Whenever my phone rang and it was her, she was either crying about what he'd done to her or she was sad about how her life was going. My heart often dropped when the phone rang as I wondered if today would be the day I'd get the news that Ebony succumbed to her pain. Just as I'd imagined, the call I once dreaded had come.

I couldn't help but wonder if I had manifested her death and blamed myself for not being there or doing enough to save her. The truth is that Ebony was born into pain and she died in pain, essentially leaving this world the same way she came into it. She was dying to live and living only to die. From a young age, Ebony struggled with the absence of our mother in her life.

Unlike me and Mallory, who had been abandoned and left in the hospital, Ebony spent the first six months of her life with my mother, building one of the most important attachments in her life. I was often resentful of Ebony because while her first moments on earth were captured, Mallory and I didn't have any baby pictures to prove our existence. Furthermore, I was under the assumption that my mother cared for Ebony because she had a lighter complexion than my brother and me. He and I were darker-skinned and were born impacted by my mother's drug use, while Ebony was not.

But I soon realized that pictures can only say a thousand words, and I saw firsthand how our mother's absence in Ebony's life negatively impacted her.

A Domino Effect

Ebony's life path mirrored that of my mother; in so many ways, she reflected my mother's life as she tried to cope. My mother was a sex worker but described herself as a prostitute, a line of work that my father used to gain power over her. Ebony walked in similar footsteps when she was trafficked by her abuser outside her independent living home—where young people can go after they age out of care—at the age of nineteen. Just like my mother, Ebony was in a domestic violence situation with a man who was old enough to be her father. Those who grew up in foster care are not strangers to rejection, abandonment, substance abuse, and homelessness. Ebony fell right in, trying to find love in an environment where it never existed, never being able to escape such a toxic cycle. She fell right into a volcano that was about to erupt.

As I sit and ponder the many ways I could have helped Ebony, I am overcome with guilt. *If I had just seen her right after her surgery, if I had called her more often, maybe she would still be here*, I find myself thinking. Biting at my fingertips as tears stream down my face, I wonder how I could have been more of a big sister to her. Ebony was stubborn and made it difficult, insisting on doing things her own way. If she asked you for advice, it was best to keep it to yourself because she would often do the opposite.

Deep down inside, I was aware Ebony made a choice to end her life, but I often question whether she really wanted to die. "I am tired," continued to ring in my ear as I listened to her last words, feeling numb as I stood in my mother's room sifting, swiping through her phone, looking through pictures, text messages, and videos—anything that would help me make sense of what appeared at the time to be sudden death.

Damn, Sis—why couldn't you just sleep off your pain? I wondered in the days following her death. *I know sleep makes me feel better. Sleep couldn't just help heal you? Did you really have to go that far to end your life?*

"It Was Her Choice"

A few months later I was talking to my mom after learning from my therapist that I was wrestling with survivor's guilt. I struggled to understand why I was here and my sister wasn't. How was it that I achieved so much success and she didn't get to fully live out her dreams?

"Mom, my therapist told me I'm struggling with survivor's guilt, and it's been hard to not feel guilty for being alive."

She quickly interjected, as she often did when confronted with uncomfortable emotions. "Ebony made her choice," she said pointedly, striking a nerve as if a stingray had just grabbed hold of my heart—because deep down, I blamed my mom for Ebony's death.

"It's your fault," I wanted to say so badly. "This was actually your choice . . . you caused her to die. If you had just given Ebony the attention she so desperately craved from you, she would still be here. But no, you laughed, joked, and made fun of her in front of her face, demonizing the lifestyle choices she made all because she wanted to be just like you."

But I didn't have the courage to say it, because my mom's comebacks were brutal and filled with so much defense. While I knew I hadn't been the perfect sister, Ebony and I resolved what we could before her death; my mom had not.

It's been four years since her death, and throughout this grieving experience I've slowly realized that the blame I so badly wanted to place on my mother really belonged to the child welfare system.

The child welfare system deemed my mother incapable of being responsible enough to care for us, so they took on that responsibility when they took permanent custody of us. The child welfare system failed Ebony, left her vulnerable instead of protecting her. She is just a microcosm of what the entire child welfare system represents for youth who are removed from their homes, in permanent custody, and who age out without guidance, protection, and love.

Ripple Effect: A Call to Action

Children enter foster care for rescue from neglect and abuse, only to be re-traumatized and re-victimized through a poorly run system. In search of love, Ebony gravitated to a father figure who abused and exploited her. Using substances to numb her pain contributed to her being homeless and lost to the streets, becoming another lost child in the world.

The child welfare system rips children away from their families only to place them in a cruel cycle that focuses more on sending out checks to foster parents than wellness checks for vulnerable children in need. Ebony should still be here, and I am angry that she isn't. While part of me recognizes she is better off, there are so many young people who go through the foster care system experiencing a lifetime of trauma only to enter into a world that wasn't meant to hold their pain. The sadness that weeps over me leaves me feeling like I've been swallowed up by the ocean, unable to breathe. I just want my sister to be here with me, though I know she is free from the world's pain and judgment.

As a teenager, I knew it was difficult to be separated from my sister, but I wasn't aware of the full impact separation had on my siblings. During bath times as children, we created an unbreakable bond as we swam, pretending we were scuba divers, talking about nonsense and washing each other's backs and faces. The soapy water held three motherless children in pain. In the depths of this water, I searched for love because that is where love first found me: My understanding of love first came from my siblings.

Now I live with the traumatic grief of the loss of my sister, recognizing that while she made a choice to disconnect from her pain, the foster care system did not take the time to help aid her in her struggles, leaving her to make a choice no person should ever have to make. Ebony is just a symbol and an example of what it's like when the child welfare system gives up on you.

One of the most incredible things my sister did was speak life to me in the midst of her pain. Ebony was the first person to tell me, "Sis, always remember that you are the prize," during a really difficult period in my life. Ebony was also the prize, and as a system, we collectively have to work to make sure that every young person knows that they are the prize despite what they've been through.

We need to put more preventative services in place so that young people know they are at the forefront and not an afterthought when it comes to creating effective and sustainable policies. If society believes that children are gifts from God, then we have to ensure, with every measure we take, young people have the ability to see themselves in spite of their pain.

Even though my birth was not planned and I came into this world with strikes already against me, I've spent my life learning that I am the prize in spite of the trauma that I've experienced. Ebony showed me that even though her life wasn't perfect and she did not hit the supposed "markers of success" in the way society defines them, her protection, love, and care over my life showed me differently. I wonder what it would have looked like or what her life would have become if society saw her as the prize.

Here is what I wish I could tell her, and what I hope she knew that I felt before she left this world.

Sis, You Were the Prize!

To Ebony: Demonized, shamed, and verbally, physically, and emotionally attacked from all angles—I understand why you felt you needed to rest. I just wish you were able to rest for a period of time and get back up. Never in a million years would I think your resting place would be in a grave six feet below the ground.

I thought I understood death, but I never fully comprehended it until I lost you. It feels like it was just yesterday when our family stood beside your bedside as you took your final breath. Even though you were tired, you fought to the very end. Doctors continued to resuscitate you as your ribs cracked, bearing the weight of their hands on your chest. I knew your exhaustion, but I still wanted to carry you to the finish line. We started on this path together. I envisioned our lives together. We would raise our kids together. You, our brother, and me. We were a unit. Our bond was unbreakable. No one could shake us.

I remember flying in from California, hoping you would wait for me. You held on. Thank you for that.

"Sis, can you hear me? Can you pull through for me? I need you," I said as I squeezed your lifeless hand. You gave no response.

You were always my protector. Who would protect me now? No one could talk badly about me except you, and rarely did you do that. You held me on a pedestal and saw little wrong with me. I think you saw me as perfect. I know you wanted so badly to be just like me, but the truth is, *I* wanted so badly to be like you. I envy the resilience you had. Your day could have been horrible, but you still took the time to see how I was doing. You often checked in with others before you checked in with yourself. Sometimes it bothered me. You took such great care of other people, but they did not always return that same consideration.

When I came out to you, I told you someone had played with my emotions. I cried, and you quickly interjected and said: "Sis, always remember that you are the prize; you are the bomb." You knew how much I struggled with self-confidence. Instead of making me feel bad about it, you continued to build me up.

Sis, I am devastated you're gone. It doesn't feel real or right. Who am I supposed to call when I need sisterly advice or just want to hear your voice? We would spend hours on the phone cracking up about everything under the sun, and I will always remember that. You tried so hard to protect my feelings, which meant you didn't share the more difficult parts of your life. You knew I'd worry. Am I selfish for wanting to know how you could end your life knowing I would feel so lost without you?

I'm deeply sorry for not seeing you before you had your surgery. You asked, but our brother wouldn't let me use his car because his tires weren't safe for the drive, and I was angry with him for that.

But I must admit that I felt anxious about where you were staying. I feared your abuser. I didn't want him to hurt me in the ways he hurt you. I never knew this would be the last time I saw you. I regret the day you called needing money and I couldn't help in the way I wanted to because I was a penniless graduate student. I also knew you might give him the money, and I didn't want that.

I would give anything to have you back. But would bringing you back on earth stop the pain you dealt with here? I just wished you knew how much people loved you. I wish we could have all shown up to support you in the ways you needed and wanted as so many did at your funeral. I will never forget our father coming to the hospital and wiping your eyes and holding you. The truth is, that's all you had ever wanted from him: to be there with you. Not just in death, but in life, and he showed up at the very end.

I hope you have the peace you so badly craved. I hope you are resting. I hope you are no longer in pain. I hope you are sleeping on a bed filled with infinite love. I hope you know that I will continue to fight for you so no other young person has to experience the level of pain you did. I want every young person to know that they deserve to live a life full of joy and fulfillment.

Thank you for breathing life into me. Thank you for telling me how beautiful I am. Thank you for looking beyond my mistakes and for giving me a chance to reconnect with you. Thank you for being selfless and honorable. I will forever miss being on the phone and hearing you say, "Hold on, Sis," so you could help someone in need. I will forever miss being by your side.

Lastly, I will forever be grateful for the times we had together. The moments of laughter, tears, countless complaints, and the memories we've shared are irreplaceable. You've spoken life to me in death, darkness, and light. Thank you for the words of encouragement you left with me.

Most importantly, you taught me that it's okay to protect myself and stand up for what's right. You taught me that it's okay to speak words of affirmation to myself in the ways you used to. Thank you for paving the way for me. You wanted that for yourself but couldn't get there. For that, I will live a life that represents the way you wanted to live while making the world a better place through your vision.

I love you, Eb, with all my heart. I am forever your sister's keeper.

YOU ARE THE PRIZE

An Unforeseen Beginning

How did I get here? Months before, I was at the pinnacle of my career. I'd just graduated with my master's from the National Urban Fellows program and was on my way to a successful job when the news of Ebony's death shook me. I also spent years working so hard on my mental health, going to therapy and thriving without medication, and now I can't even get out of bed?

I thought I would be unfazed by the aftermath of Ebony's death, thinking I'd gone through much more and that surely I was going to get through this with no problems. I soon realized that wasn't true. I wasn't aware of the early signs of grief and depression. I just knew that I was spending more time in my bed than I was with friends and loved ones. I felt like I was lying in a dark hole.

Lying in my bed for weeks, enfolded under the blankets with the blinds and doors shut and clinging to my pillow, unable to move, I waited for the sparkle in my eye to return. Motivation escaped me, and that was certainly rare. One moment I was fine, and then suddenly I was clenching my chest the panic staying longer than usual. All I wanted to do was cry because I thought I was dying.

"The sparkle in your eyes left when your sister died," kept ringing in my ears as I visualized my ex-partner's words bannering across my face. It felt as if my world came crumbling down and I didn't know where to turn but to find comfort in my pillow.

Ebony died years ago and the remnants of her death don't leave me; it feels as though it just happened yesterday. Mornings have become much harder. I stand in the kitchen pouring a glass of water, then I suddenly run to the bathroom, vomiting from the nausea-inducing anxiety sitting in the pit of my stomach. And then those sleepless nights when I toss and turn, trying to escape from nightmare after nightmare only to find that my alarm clock has gone off and I can't even turn over to press the snooze button—on those days, I try to pull myself out of bed, but I can't.

How come no one tells you what grief is like or how much loss can impact a person? I'm tired. The cycle of self-hate continues to intrude on my mind. My room looks like a special edition of a *Hoarders* episode airing on TLC. Piles of clothes lay everywhere as if a tornado just stormed through. I didn't realize the bedroom floor was an actual reflection of how my life feels.

Crossroads

I found myself at one of the most critical points in my life, as if I stood at the center of the universe figuring out which direction to go in. I was supposed to be attending an anticipated conference on child welfare, during which I would debut the Courageous Conversations series I helped create in honor of Ebony and the hundreds of thousands young people in foster care. I couldn't quite navigate how I could fly all the way to Boston in the state I was in.

"I'm really concerned about you; we need to get you some help," my therapist shared.

The sense of urgency behind her words made me feel as though something was really wrong. Quickly setting up an appointment with the Intensive Outpatient Treatment program at Kaiser, I found myself feeling stuck. Do I go and appease them and reject what my body is saying, or do I stay back and take care of myself?

Taking care of myself wasn't instilled in me. I grew up learning that I needed to care for others in order to receive and maintain love while neglecting myself in the process. The inner turmoil I was experiencing could no longer be ignored. I was at a crossroads, forced to make a decision between presenting at a high-stakes national conference or giving myself the care I needed and deserved. During my intake appointment with the IOP therapist, he pointed out I was struggling with an enormous amount of guilt and shame. I decided to take the plunge, cancel my flight to Boston, and attend the IOP program.

I Will Arrive

We love to overemphasize the importance of persistence, resilience, and determination, but we don't acknowledge the faint breaths people take each day competing with the internal force of our lungs that cannot easily keep up.

I toss and turn in the middle of the night with a pounding heartbeat, reliving pieces of my childhood nightmares that don't ever seem to go away. While much of the world wakes up and stretches and breathes, my body wakes up with buried pain crouched on top of me.

"How am I going to get through this day?" I ask myself, wondering which mask I need to wear in order to show up.

Dear little Black girl, you swam to the depths of the ocean in search of love, and it was there that you found yourself.

The truth is, as a young person who experiences the foster care system, you don't get a chance to take breaks. You spend your childhood experiencing a lifetime of trauma only to grow into an adult and realize you have to spend your adulthood piecing together the misery of your youth. How *unfair!*

With the influence of Christianity on my life, I learned very early that I needed to quickly let things go and keep moving forward despite any obstacles that were set before me, so I did that until I couldn't do it anymore.

What I soon realized was that I was not only suppressing the things I was going through and operating from a place of functional depression and anxiety, but I was putting pressure on myself to succeed when all I ever wanted to do was sleep the pain away. In the midst of doing all the "right things," such as obtaining my high school diploma, my undergraduate degree, and then my graduate degree, I bought into the lie that having degrees meant that life would be better. While life has been easy in some respects, I can't ignore the unspoken traumas I live through on a daily basis as a Black, queer woman.

I experience a knee jerk reaction when I hear things like, "Some things that break cannot be fixed." My automatic response wants to say that everything that breaks can be fixed without ignoring the complexity of how we define what's broken.

Why is it easier for the human mind to make sense of the fact that people who are paralyzed may never be able to walk again than it is for the possibility that someone who has experienced trauma might not heal? Is it okay if things do not heal? Do all things actually heal? Or have we created modifications to visually please society because we cannot grasp that some things are just imperfect? It's okay to build modifications for those who need them, but why do we get to decide who needs these modifications as if having a few cracks is horrible? Maybe this is why I can't stand to visit my own scars on my body, as they remind me that I am no longer this perfect or whole being. Is this the reason why I begrudgingly hold my breath when I see my nephew scrape up his perfect little knee without recognizing his journey toward that wound?

I miss the blissful laughter I hear coming out of his mouth as he runs toward the wind of freedom because it reminds me of when I was once that child. Mallory, Ebony, and I would crawl on our knees around the house, wistfully enjoying our game of tag, until I abruptly heard in the distance: "If you keep crawling on your knees, they are going to turn black."

The notion of turning darker was haunting, and even though her words didn't matter at the moment while we kept crawling, the reminiscence of her words lay beneath my conscience. Subconsciously, I hated my knees and any wounds that permanently tattooed my body. So when I look at my knees, I don't see the playful carefree girl; I see the results of not listening to Granma when she said, "Stop crawling on your knees."

But I am someone who experienced lasting trauma in the womb, and thirty years later I am much better off than how society said I would be—but they've also ignored the fact that I am still human.

Yes, I've worked at the White House. Yes, I've written policy reports to get congressional leaders and the public to give attention to a pressing need. I'm also exhausted, weary, sad, and I feel like I am not allowed to grieve.

The period I spent at IOP gave me a reason to wake up because I could just show up in a place full of strangers and just be me. Nothing more, nothing less. If there was any pressure for me to be perfect, it was because of myself. I was given permission to feel all of my feelings within boundaries of course, but I was allowed to feel the good, the bad, the ugly, and the indifferent. At times it wasn't easy because my mind clung to the many times I was told that my feelings were not real and didn't matter.

Part of the reason why many people don't allow themselves to feel their feelings is because of fear. So many of us have been told when we've cried to "stop crying" or "I'll give you something to cry about," shutting down the feelings behind why we were crying in the first place, stuffing them deeper and covering them with remorse. Words have a lasting impact, and while I was at IOP, I was given tools each day to help disprove the things that have tried to define me.

EPILOGUE

Healing Is a Lifelong Journey

Attending IOP was one of the best decisions I've made for myself. It gave me a chance to be human again. While it was intimidating to put myself out there when I looked across the room at my fellow classmates, I finally saw myself. I saw the years of pain, shame, guilt, and feelings of unworthiness among us.

But as I continued to unpack those internal feelings, I saw a path. I saw people picking up their heads truly feeling their inner emotions, which gave me the space to also see myself. When I saw the staff effortlessly show up day by day with gratitude, I knew that I was in good hands because I was healing in the community.

On the last day of the program I was handed a Certification of Completion. While I knew it was only the beginning, I said this to the group before leaving:

"Thank you for showing up each day with an aura of hope. Thank you for walking with me and the group, starting off each topic and workshop by asking us what our strengths are. Thank you for setting the tone for safety each day, which allowed me to fully engage and be myself without fear of judgement.

To my therapist Charles: Thank you for being a rockstar. Thank you for being a pillar of light and truth. Thank you for showing up when I needed to talk, and most importantly, thank you for looking into my eyes and recognizing that I, too, am worthy of all good things. As a child I used to walk with my head down, but each day with you I was reminded that I belong.

One of the last things Ebony said to me was, "Sis, always remember that you are the prize." She wanted me to remember these words when she was alive, and now she wants me to carry those words with her in her place of rest. I want to remind each of us that we, too, are the prize. The world may have been harsh to us, and we may have even been harsh with ourselves.

As I pass her words off to you, I want you to remember that there is light in and within you. I want us to remember that healing is a lifelong journey. I want us to remember that it's okay to not be okay. It's okay for us to feel all things. It's okay for us to feel angry, sad, uncertain, powerless, frozen, and everything in between.

It's also okay to peel back the callouses (like the dry crust on our feet) and shave away the traumas of our past and present. I want us to remember that it's also okay to dream, it's okay for us to hold ourselves when we feel alone, and it's okay for us to lift up our heads and let some of the light in—because as I see each of you, I see me. And when I see me, I see the dim light getting brighter and becoming a place that I can finally come home to.

I am coming home to myself and so are each of us. So as we navigate through the waters, remember that it is okay to set our worries on the leaf and allow it to wither away. And when those thoughts come back, it's okay to revisit those feelings, because those feelings are what help carry us through. Just like the tree that has deep roots, those roots blossom and turn into leaves that disconnect and fall to the ground as new ones appear. Allow our new leaves to appear as they remind us of the beauty of growth. We are the tree of life, full of bravery and courage.

Each day may not be a good day, but it's a day that we have to come back to ourselves. So as we continue this journey together, let's always remember that *we are the prize*!

Before I walked out the door of the IOP community, I read to them one last thing that I want all of us to remember as we all experience our own pivotal moments in this lifetime. This is your assignment:

Feel all the things. Feel the hard things. The inexplicable things, the things that make you disavow humanity's capacity for redemption. Feel all the maddening paradoxes. Feel overwhelmed and crazy. Feel uncertain. Feel angry. Feel afraid. Feel powerless. Feel frozen—and then *focus*.

Pick up your pen. Pick up your paintbrush. Pick up your damn chin. Put your two calloused hands on the turntables, in the clay, on the strings. Get behind the camera. Look for that pinprick of light. Look for the truth (yes, it is a thing—it still exists).

Focus on that light. Enlarge it. Reveal the fierce urgency of now. Reveal how shattered we are, how capable of being repaired. But don't lament the break. Nothing new would be built if things were never broken. A wise man once said: There's a crack in everything. That's how the light gets in. Get after that light.

This is your assignment (Martin, 2017).

ACKNOWLEDGMENTS

To my late Great Aunt affectionately known as Granma: I want to thank you for instilling in me the importance of love, generosity, compassion, and family. Because of you, I am connected to my biological family in ways I never would've been if it wasn't for you. As overwhelming as it was, I appreciate you taking my siblings and me in and keeping us together; you preserved our relationship. To my late sister Ebony: I want to thank you for your unfailing love for me. Thank you for telling me I am the prize. Without you, this book wouldn't exist. To my late father, I know life wasn't always easy for you. Thank you for reminding me of my brilliance in the midst of your own struggles. In honor of Rebecca Weichand, Baby Kenai, and my other ancestors and angels: Thank you for watching over me.

To my mother, thank you for choosing to give me the gift of life even when life hasn't always been a gift.

To my emotional support animal, Biscuits and Gravy, Bella, and Buttercup: Thank you for the light, love, and presence you all add to my life. Your unconditional love has shown me how to accept love, and that means more to me than you all will ever know.

To my best friend, Scarlett: You've been there with me from the very beginning of my transformation, and you continue to be there for me every step of the way. You've walked this journey called life with me, and I am thankful for you every day. Thank you for being a consistent support in my life. I love you.

To my siblings: There is no greater relationship than the sibling bond. Thank you to each of you for being a part of my journey through the ups, downs, challenges, and wins of life. To my lifeline, Mallory: I want to thank you for being a source of protection in my life. As children we created an unbreakable bond, and as life has brought us through tremendous hardships, you've been there.

To my nieces, Amira, Amina, Harmony, Elizabeth, Maya, and Sofia, and my nephews, Kyheem, Anthony Jr, Jamel, Khaidyn, Josiah, and Jordan: Aunty loves you all so much. You all give me a reason to live, and I am blessed to be your Aunty.

To my aunts, uncles, and cousins, thank you for your unwavering wisdom and love. To my Aunty Linda, I want to thank you for your care, love, and generosity in my life. Even though you had four children of your own, you took my siblings and me in and showed us what family was all about.

To my Charles Street AME church family and Pastor Rev. Gregory and Barbara Groover: You watched me grow up from a young girl to an adult. The leadership you've displayed throughout the years speaks volumes. You instilled in me the importance of generosity, love, spirituality, and community. Because of your love, I am who I am today.

To my high school administrators, Mr. Downing and Dr. Ferrer: Thank you for believing in me when I didn't believe in myself. You saw my potential before I did and decided to invest. I am forever grateful for your consistent mentorship in my life.

To my college professors, Professor Scott Nowka, Dr. Ivy George, Dr. Judith Oleson, Professor Sybil Coleman, Dr. Margaret Deweese-Boyd, Dr. Daniel Johnson, and last but not least to the late Dr. James Trent: I want to thank you for seeing me beyond the imperfections of my trauma. Thank you for helping me cultivate my love for knowledge.

To Ivette Diaz, thank you for meeting me where I was. As a recent student who found myself homeless during one of the most critical times in my life, you provided opportunities to me that not only helped me survive but thrive.

To my impromptu editing team, Chris Foreman, Christine Ristaino, Jennifer Grady, John Kelly, Jane Krieke, Julio Rodriquez, Mary Fernandi, Marcia Hopkins, Ruth McRoy, Susan Kooperstein, and all others who contributed toward this process, my love for you runs deep. Thank you for your endless support, lending your ideas to brainstorm with me, and for always being available and ready to help when I needed it.

To Lyd Nenmo, thank you for helping me design my book cover in collaboration with New Degree Press. I will always remember when you first reached out and offered to support me in whatever way possible, offering your generosity and time to develop this beautiful concept.

To my author and beta reader community, and all those who've supported me through purchasing my memoir, sharing a kind word of encouragement—thank you for holding me in love during this time.

Kent Downing, Rianna Bazzinotti, Trinity Badding, Renee Hulett, Ruth McRoy, Eliza Jones, tagriffen, Paola Garcia, C Allison John, Maurice B. Wright, Sarah Bennice Gentle, Michaela Smith, Samantha Taylor, Ayana Corbin Minor, Sharon Manning, Lynette Holmes, Christine Hill,

Jessica James, Linda Dorch, Rolanda Dudley- Cowans, Diana Ortega, Joe Nelson, Arnold Chandler, Kayla Morgan, Stephanie Francis, Jason Price, Rafael Lopez, Emily Wymore, Gennie Musau, Rachel Carroll, Joanna Gallagher, Mika Jax, Kayla Schwanke, Sandra Morris, Peter Kang, Scarlett Foston, Sanders Royal, Mark and Gina Lyon, Patricia Hainey, Alexandra McFadden, Kathleen Joof, Emilee Pihi, Sarah Tang, Kaylia Ferguson, Mario Nash, Briana Osbourne, Russ Finkelstein, Elle Unique, Robin Selwitz, Maddy Ullman, Lauren Tilmont, Alyssa Acton, Angel Nguyen, S.Marienau Turpin, Jasmine M. Ganter, Adrienne Carmack, Jenifer Maze, Maryellen Santiago, John Noble, Beth Fraker, Helen Ellis, Kerry Howington, Barbara Ferrer, Wendy MacNaughton, S. Scheff, Susan Stoebner, Susan Kooperstein, Lael Morris, Dr.Elizabeth A. Thompson, Sarah Rosenstein, Jennifer Ogden, Alexis and Robert Lambert, Jessica Hunkler, SC Brooks, Elizabeth Currie-Wand, Mahyrah Shamseddine, Winnie Wechsler, Emily Satifka, Amber Woods, Bryan Imke, Ethan Kilgore, Professor Sybil W. Coleman, Mary Bissell, Austin Hanlin, Lida Hamilton, Lisa Spinali, Becky Monroe, Patricia Lester, Lydia Nenno, JLH Demers, Elizabeth Leitzmann, Dorothy Boorse, Molly Ptaszek, Ithar Gabriel, Helen Schoonmaker, Becky Freemal, Tanisha Abernathy, Nerissa E. Smith, Tamiesha Lawrence, Catie Buckingham, Stephanie Clark, Jackie Gannon, Roy Austin, Mary Greiner, Sarah Sessa, Jeanna Pritzker, Moira Szilagyi, Ruth Boys, Haydee Adelita, Devin Brown, Everett Thomas, Ronesha Williams, Natalie Giordano, Rebecca Dowling Alvarez, Carlee Welsh, Laura Crimaldi, Joy Finneran, Megan Clarke, Jane Halladay Goldman, Dele Lowman Smith, LaToya Johnson, Daniel Heimpel, John Kelly, Shanna Fishel, Tiffany Morris, John McDonough, Marcia

Myers Sprinstead, Sixto Cancel, Ktuta Shinda?, Anna Gennari, Wilondja Muyoma, Elizabeth Speck, Serena Gilchrist, Allison Coble, Yali Lincroft, Mary Lapka, Cheri Crossman, Savonna Stender, Kimberly Murtaugh, Kaitlin C. Tapia, Jennifer Grady, Ellen Howard-Cooper, Stacy Strobel, Katherina Ouellette, RoseMary Covington, Taylor Draddy, Rebecca Shaw, Pamela Morales, Malkior Rivera Allison Lyon, Kristen Tenglin, Ana Payson, Elizabeth Norcini, Alena Casey, Vikki Rompala, Maria Rose, Sarah Ruvo, Megan Kyle, Elizabeth Lyon, Sarah Jane Forman, Jane Krienke, Aude Guerrucci, Laurie T. Ruschel, Sandra Ryan, Patti Bayross, Stefanie Cruz, Erika Tullberh, Laura Donworth, Ivette Diaz, Abbie Weaber, Leslie Borkenhagen, Jordan Equitable Luke, Julie Shapiro, Rachel Birmingham, Jordan Waterwash, Chris Foreman, Christina Parker, Leah Glasheen, Lindsey Harrington, J Carley Flores-Adams, Carli Rhoades, Patrice Davis, Erinn Wong, Ashley Cole McCullough, Matthew Charles Davis, Christen JK, Kimberly Biddle, Tracie Sullivan, Heather Clifford, Christine Ristaino, Caitlin Belley, Zoey Meyer-Jens, Alyssa Barkley, Shante B, Rebecca Finney, Jenny Lai, Jo Lin, Jessie Coffman, Danielle Johnson, Mary Elizabeth Frediani, Mary Speta, Mandie Wilson, Cherilyn Tiongson, Eric Koester, CT Tranchell, Amelia Vierstra, Elvin Ortiz, Sabriya Dillard, Sade Daniels, Dee Bonnick, Judy Cockerton, Jenna Rose Mackenzie, Adrianne Denenberg, Janelle Turner, Leah Serao Battillo, Becca Fipphen, Serene King, Andrea Clifford, Rodney Walker, Megan Lestino, Mallory Morris, Lydia Nenno, Tnertj, Christy Singleton, Abigail Durant, Shariann Coombs, Melissa Foye, Sajena Cartagena, Stacie Finlayson, Mackenzie Olsen, Elliott Orrin Hinkle, Crystal Welch, Samantha Berg, Kioina Myers, Vanessa Hernandez,

Mari Itzkowitz, Rachel Albaugh, Catherine Boynton, Alexis Burger, Okererra Mills, Ravenell, and Cedric Riley.

Lastly, I want to send a huge thank you to the New Degree Press team, especially Professor Eric Koester, Brian Biles, Jordan Waterwash, Chelsea Friday, Linda Beradelli, Stephanie Mckibben, and John Saunders. Through the rain, storm, sunshine, and rainbows, you all have been there for me every step of the way. Thank you for standing by me.

I cannot express my deepest gratitude for each of you who have supported me on this journey. If I've not mentioned you it is not because you have not touched my heart; it is because of human error. Please do always remember that you are the prize.

APPENDIX

Metamorphosis

Dettlaff, Alan, Kristen Weber, Maya Pendleton, Reiko Boyd, Bill Bettencourt, and Leonard Burton. "It is Not a Broken System, It is a System that Needs to be Broken: The upEND Movement to Abolish the Child Welfare System." *Journal of Public Child Welfare* 14 no. 5 (September 2020): 500-517.

The Annie E. Casey Foundation: Kids Count Data Center. "Child population by race in the United States." Accessed January 23, 2021. https://datacenter.kidscount.org/data/tables/103-child-population-by-race?loc=1&loct=1#detailed/1/any/false/574,1729,37,871,870,573,869,36,868,867/68,69,67,12,70,66,71,72/423,424

The Annie E. Casey Foundation: Kids Count Data Center. "Children in foster care by race and Hispanic origin in the United States." Accessed January 23, 2021. https://datacenter.kidscount.org/data/tables/6246-children-in-foster-care-by-race-and-hispanic-origin?loc=1&loct=1#detailed/1/any/false/1729,37,871,870,573,869,36,868,867,133/2638,2601,2600,2598,2603,2597,2602,1353/12992,12993

Child Welfare Information Gateway. (2021). Child Welfare Practice to Address Racial Disproportionality and Disparity. US Department of Health and Human Services, Administration

for Children and Families, Children's Bureau. https://www.
childwelfare.gov/pubs/issue-briefs/racial-disproportionality

Welch, Morgan, Ron Haskins. "What COVID-19 Means for
America's Child Welfare System." *Brookings*, April 30, 2020.
https://www.brookings.edu/research/what-covid-19-means-
for-americas-child-welfare-system/

Chapter 12: Turning Point

"After a Diagnosis." Mental Health America, accessed September
26, 2020. https://www.mhanational.org/after-diagnosis

Capps, Charles. *God's Creative Power Will Work for You*. Tulsa:
Harrison House, 1976

"Mental Health by the Numbers." National Alliance on Mental
Illness, accessed September 26, 2020. https://nami.org/mhstats

Meyer, Joyce. *Beauty for Ashes: Receiving Emotional Healing*. New
York: Warner Faith, 2003.

Chapter 13: Monumental Figure

Grassley, Chuck. "Floor Statement of Sen. Chuck Grassley on
Foster Youth and an Individual Experience." Speech, Washington, DC, July 7, 2014. https://www.grassley.senate.gov/
news/news-releases/floor-statement-sen-chuck-grassley-fos-
ter-youth-and-individual-experience

Chapter 14: The Peak

AFCARS data, US Children's Bureau, Administration for Children, Youth and Families: Trends in Foster Care & Adoption:
FY 2010- 2019. (November 8, 2018). https://www.acf.hhs.gov/
cb/report/trends-foster-care-adoption-2019

Congressional Coalition on Adoption Institute. "Shaping Tomor-
row with Today's Minds: Applying Updated Solutions to an

Outdated System." 2014. http://s3.amazonaws.com/ccai-website/2014_CCAI_Foster_Youth_Internship_Report.pdf

Chapter 15: The White House

Greeson, J. K., E. C. Briggs, C. L. Kisiel, C. M. Layne, G. S. Ake III, S. J. Ko, and J. A. Fairbank. (2011). Complex Trauma and Mental Health in Children and Adolescents Placed in Foster Care: Findings from the National Child Traumatic Stress Network. Child Welfare, 90(6), 91-108.

Chapter 20

Shirk Stangler. *What Happens to Kids When They Age out of the Foster Care System?* (Boulder: Westview Press, 2004.)

Healing Is a Lifelong Journey

Martin, Courtney and Wendy MacNaughton. *Focus.* 2017. Art print. https://society6.com/product/focus-2017-by-courtney-martin-and-wendy-macnaughton_print